NO SWEAT
PUBLIC
SPEAKING!

How to **Develop, Practice,** and **Deliver** a
Knock Your Socks Off Presentation!
with *No Sweat!*

FRED E. MILLER

Illustrated by David Zamudio

No Sweat Public Speaking! How to **Develop, Practice** and **Deliver** a Knock Your Socks Off Presentation! With *No Sweat!*

Published by Fred Co., St. Louis, MO.

To order additional copies of this title, contact your local bookstore or go to nosweatpublicspeaking.com.

The author may be contacted thru his website nosweatpublicspeaking.com.

Cover Design by Sarah Barrie, Business Couture, www.bizcouture.com.
Illustrations by David Zamudio, Zamudio Art Studios, www.zamudiosartstudio.com.

Printed in the United States of America.

First Printing, 2011.

ISBN-13: 978-0-9843967-0-2
Library of Congress Control Number: 2011921744

1. Public Speaking 2. Presentations 3. Business

Contents

Acknowledgements

The ability to deliver speeches and make presentations is a skill that is learned.

We are not born with expertise to do this. I *guarantee* I wasn't!

We must *learn* how to:
- Develop a Presentation
- Practice a Presentation
- Deliver a Presentation

Learning all this does not happen quickly. It is a process.

While much of it is self study and observation, I would not have the knowledge and competence I have today were it not for great advice and encouragement from many.

Toastmasters is the organization I must first acknowledge. Their structured, progressive program for learning the fundamentals of Public Speaking was extremely helpful. I was fortunate to find a club that was a good fit for me. For many years I attended Tarsus Toastmasters in Clayton, Missouri. It's been quite a while since I was present at a meeting, but many memories and friendships remain. I'm sure I'll miss a few names, but want to mention: Sabine Robinson, Jim Salih, Sharon Winstein, John Stuckey, Paul Dugo, Paul Lore, Kapano Allmon, Norbert and Helmi Mason, Nancy Higgins, Richard McCollum, Mitch Markow, Donna Raedake, Nick Greles, David Cotton, Bruce Lucas, Wanda Gordon, Glenn Knudson, Bobbi Linkemer, Dave Moore, Shannon Whitaker, and Don Meldrum.

My wife, Beverly, has heard (should I say, endured) more of my presentations than a human should be subjected to. (Some of them while *trapped* in a car speeding down a highway.) Her encouragement and suggestions helped me work and rework presentations that were not ready for prime time. Being an educator, and teaching Pubic Speaking to her students, was a great benefit to me. I am indebted to her!

I owe special thanks to two great friends, Jennifer Tobias and Russ Henneberry. Each has been beyond generous in giving me their time and expert help. Both have been mentors to me in the writing and production of this book and the website, www.nosweatpublicspeaking.com. Without their advice and encouragement, this project might never have been completed. Jennifer also did final editing for me which was sorely needed after I made numerous additions and changes.

A thanks for encouragement also goes to Joe High, Dale Furtwengler, Mike Rohan, David Zamudio, Dan Dobinsky, Cathy Sexton, Tom Terrific, Fred Firestone, Monroe Smith, Tom Ruwitch, Steve Barcellona, Michael Bitter, and Ron Amen.

Mary Menke, one of my editors, put up with my procrastination, repetition, and skilled butchering of the English language. She gets a big, "Thank You!" for a job well done.

ACKNOWLEDGEMENTS

Sarah Barrie, Business Couture, www.bizcouture.com, designed the book cover, back cover and did the layout work. She is professional, easy to work with, and provided much needed expert advice and support.

Finally, I owe much to the many speakers who:
- Don't write their own Introduction.
- Write their own Introduction, but poorly so.
- Don't have a Strong Opening to their Presentations.
- Don't have great Content.
- Have great Content, but don't Deliver it Well.
- Take Questions *after* Closing their talk.
- Have non-memorable Closings.
- Deliver Nonverbal Communication that is not in sync with their Verbal Communication.
- Who use line after line after line of bullet points in a slide presentation, and read each of them to their audience.
- Who use slides with a font so small it can't be read.
- Use props incorrectly.
- Distribute handouts *before* they speak so the audience can read *with* the speaker, *behind* the speaker, and *ahead* of the speaker.
- Use "ahhs" and "errs" and other fillers when they should be pausing and making no sounds.

If it were not for having done many of these things myself, multiple times, and seeing so many others do the same, I might not have written this book.

It pains me that *I* didn't know better. Many others don't know how to present their ideas.

I *know* there are *tens of thousands of presentations*, with great content for target audiences that were delivered in a way that made it almost impossible for the audience to understand and process the message. The reason for this unfortunate fact is that the speaker didn't possess the presentation skills necessary to convey their message. It's frustrating to the audience and the presenter.

I *believe* there are *thousands of presentations*, with superb content that would benefit specific audiences, yet have *never been presented*. They've never been delivered because of the Fear of Public Speaking. This is unfortunate. Their great information is never disseminated and a person's career is often held back because of this fear.

Presentation skills can be *learned!*

The Fear of Public Speaking *can be overcome.*

If fear or lack of skills is holding you back from reaching *your* goals, this book will help!

Foreword

Why Give Presentations?

Why Do Public Speaking?

When I was in Toastmasters, an International, nonprofit organization designed to help people overcome their fear of public speaking, one of my duties was to answer inquiries from people who wanted more information. They wanted to know what a typical meeting was like, who were members, what kind of training was offered, and other questions specifically relevant to our club.

I always asked how they heard about us and what they wanted to accomplish.

Many calls were like this one:

"I'm an accountant. I work more with numbers than I work with people. I do really good work, sitting in my cubicle, and working on my computer. I don't give presentations, and I don't want to. My boss told me that if I ever want to advance in this firm I'm going to have to regularly give presentations to groups of prospects, clients, and colleagues."

*"My goal is to become a partner someday.
Can Toastmasters help me?"*

Some calls went right to the heart of the matter with comments like this: "I have to make speeches and I have a fear of public speaking. I need help. What can Toastmasters offer me?"

Each time, I said it would be a great place to start, and invited them to come as a guest to the next meeting.

Many accepted my invitation, and quite a few went on to achieve their goals.

Most people, if they hope to advance in their careers, will have to speak with groups. Even if they *don't* want to climb the corporate ladder, they might be asked to present on occasion. It may *not* be optional. Just like the example of the accountant, these presentations can be internal or external.

They can be formal or informal.

Maybe not rooms filled with large audiences, but certainly smaller numbers of people.

Being able to speak in front of groups improves one-on-one communication, and I *know* you do that!

The ability to communicate well is one of the most important skills a person can possess.

I once spoke with a large group of unemployed professionals. They were from a variety of fields. My talk was about public speaking and communication. Following my presentation, a Human Resource professional spoke with the group. She talked about very talented people with great work histories, education and work ethics coming to her office and interviewing for open positions.

One of the things she found shocking was the high number of individuals who couldn't communicate well!

She had to consider that candidates for the slots she was trying to fill sometimes would have to work in teams. Occasionally, they would be expected to interact with other employees, customers, and even prospects at very crucial times.

Their *communication deficiency* greatly lowered the odds of their being hired.

I was recently coaching a person in a management position at one of the largest auditing companies in the country. She related a story to me about an individual in the company who was one of the best she knew for doing a detailed, technical audit. Unfortunately, he will probably stay in the lower company position he now occupies because of an inability to communicate well with team members, prospects and clients.

A person must know how to present to an audience in a manner that entertains, educates and explains their topic. Essentially, you could be the expert who could write the definitive book on your area of expertise, but if you can't communicate that knowledge effectively, your career will be severely stifled.

Another good reason to speak is to establish **credibility**.

There are a number of ways to get credibility. Here are a few:
- Have news and feature stories published in the media *about* you.
- *Write* articles and have them published.
- *Do Public Speaking and Give Presentations!*

Being on television and radio and having articles published about you can be accomplished, especially with the help of a good PR firm. Realistically, and something you can better control, is writing articles and making presentations.

Perception is reality. If you publish and do public speaking, you gain **credibility**.

If you have **credibility**, many consider you an expert. I don't know about you, but I certainly would rather deal with an expert. So, if people think you're an expert; your career should take off – correct?

Giving presentations is also a great **self-confidence** builder. It's kind of like, "If I can do *this*, I can do *anything!*"

Many whom find success speaking in front of groups go on to tackle other activities they have avoided. They take on behaviors outside their comfort zone because of the confidence gained through speaking and giving presentations.

Here's a fact to remember: When you step out of your comfort zone – you make it *larger!*

If you are a **leader**, people expect you to give great presentations.

If you aspire to be a leader, giving great presentations can be one of the skills that will take you to that position.

Another reason to develop the skill of public speaking is this: You have goals, opinions, points of view, feelings and thoughts you want to express, and good ideas you want to share, right? Well, the ability to do public speaking will make conveying these things to others a lot easier, won't it? (It would be a shame to keep all this great stuff to yourself!)

So, for *many* reasons, Speak and Give Presentations! – **GET IT?**

My Goal/Your Goal: For the Audience to **GET IT!**

The goal of *all* communication - verbal, written or visual - is the same.

We want the recipient, or recipients, quickly as possible, to understand our message, or actually *say*, internally or externally, **I GET IT!**

They may agree, disagree, or be somewhere between. Those scenarios are all OK.

The important thing is that they **GET IT!**

Once they've **got it**, a discussion can start taking place. (This assumes, of course, *their* interpretation of your message is the one *you* intended them to get.)

The goal of this book is that *you* **GET IT!**

The graphics and text have the **I GET IT!** goal in mind.

As just stated, you may not agree with everything I write. That's fine.

As you read this book, do as you should with most things in life that are presented to you: *Be a sponge*, absorb *everything* – and squeeze out what you don't need!

I want you to **GET IT!** so you can ask yourself good, thought-provoking questions about developing, practicing, and delivering a presentation.

My goal is that *you* will give a presentation good enough that when you close *your* talk the entire audience - **GETS IT!**

To Help You **GET IT!**
I've Included Mind Mapping

Many years ago, at an International Toastmasters convention in St. Louis, Missouri, I was introduced to **Mind Mapping.**

One of the seminars I attended was, Speaking without Notes.

No one wants to be just a talking head behind the lectern, so the title of this workshop really pulled me in. If I'm at the lectern and merely reading a speech, I'm not going to be very effective.

The session was conducted by a high school principal. He taught us a visual technique for remembering called *Pegging.* It's an excellent technique for visually remembering the elements of your speech. It consisted of 20 mental pegs that could have key words of a speech *mentally glued* to them that could be recalled while delivering a speech. It was a good lesson, and I still can recall each of those 20 pegs today.

Here are a few of those pegs:
1. Tree - Picture a tall pine
2. Light switch - On / Off
3. Three-legged stool
4. Car - Four doors or four tires
5. Glove - Five fingers

6. Six shooter cowboy gun
7. A pair of Dice (Seven come Eleven, a term used when shooting craps)
8. Skate (Eight rhymes with skate.)
9. Golf Clubs (The Ninth Hole is the Watering Hole, aka.Bar – but Golf Clubs is the image
10. Bowling Pins (Ten pins in a setup.)

The next step was to take super crazy mental glue and attach pictures of key words from the presentation on each of the pegs. **Example:** If the body of my speech was about "Prospecting," and peg number three was next, I might picture the three-legged stool in a shallow stream. I'd then mentally glue an old miner to the stool and picture him panning (prospecting) for gold. This picture would cue me to that part of my talk.

This might be a technique you can use, also.

During the question and answer session, someone asked the presenter, "How do you develop your talks?"

"Mind Mapping," was his brief reply. Then he flashed a slide on the wall that had colored lines, words, and symbols radiating from the center.

I thought to myself, "Hmm, that looks interesting!"

Then, the speaker said, "Not only do I develop my speeches with Mind Maps, I also use them to practice and deliver my talks."

"Cool!" I thought.

"Furthermore," he continued, "I gave three speeches on the same day last week, and used Mind Maps for all of them."

Wow! That did it for me! I *knew* I had to learn more about this visual tool called **Mind Mapping.**

Ever since that initial introduction, I've been studying and exploring new uses for this tool and how to get the maximum benefits from it.

My only regret about **Mind Mapping** - I didn't discover it sooner!

Mind Mapping is a visual, nonlinear, brainstorming tool that is the "*Swiss Army Knife* for the Brain."

It is one of the best ways to maximize ideas and solutions to everyday challenges and opportunities and can be applied in both personal and business areas.

Its main applications are:

- Strategic Planning
- Problem Solving
- Decision Making
- Process Development
- Writing and Presenting a Speech (**GET IT!**)
- Writing a Book (Imagine that!)
- Studying
- Other brain related activities

Mind Mapping was developed in the 1970s by the British author and educational consultant, Tony Buzan.

He found most college students, if they took class notes at all, took lousy ones that were fairly useless.

He wanted to develop something that was brief, visual, non-linear, colorful, used images, and worked by association; i.e., *note-taking the way our brains work!*

His brother, Barry, realized that if Mind Mapping is a good way to *take* notes, it might be a good way to *make* notes.

I use it for *many* things, including most applications just mentioned, plus: to-do lists, trip and event planning, website development and nearly anything else that comes to mind.

I use it to develop, practice, and deliver presentations.

I used Mind Mapping to write this book, and you'll see several examples of Mind Maps here.

The Mind Map of the entire book is at:
www.nosweatpublicspeaking.com/book/mindmap

I also have a separate site dedicated to Mind Mapping at:
www.mastermindmapper.com

One of the premises of Mind Mapping is that it brings together the left (linear or logical) side of the brain, and the right (creative) half of the brain. By using it, we can develop ideas and solutions the way our brain works.

Mind Mapping Versus Outlining

The example on the next page will illustrate the theory and benefits of Mind Mapping.

Start a project outline on a lined piece of paper by writing the headline MY PROJECT at the top.

What usually happens is that you'll stare and stare at the paper, and eventually begin to outline and write: IA, IB, etc.

After working on this for a while, you realize what's wrote for III B should be II A.

Ever happen to you?

Of course it has!

The problem is when projects, or any kind of brain activity, are done in a linear manner, or outlining, we're trying to *organize* thoughts *before they're developed!*

Our brains don't work this way!

Mind Mapping works the way our brains work! It brings together both sides of the brain.

My Project
I
A
B
C
II
A
B
III
A
B

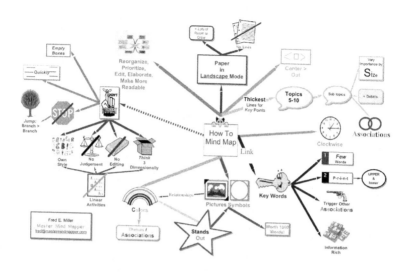

Mind Mapping Basics

- Get a sheet of large, unlined paper, and place it in the *land-scape* mode.
- This gives you *lots* of room to grow. You'll need it because so many ideas and solutions will be generated!
- Place the main subject in the middle and make it a picture or symbol.
- Generate sub-topics from the center going out.
- Start at 12:00 and go clockwise.
- Show importance by graphic or symbol, size of the type and the thickness of the lines. Larger graphics and thicker lines will be closer to the center.
- Use Key Words, words that quickly summarize your thoughts.
- Use as few words as possible because they are information-rich and will trigger other associations. Our brain thinks by associations.

- Use pictures and symbols because they *are* worth 1,000+ words.
- Add colors to show themes and associations.
- Do it quickly and without being judgmental (there are no "bad" ideas).
- Go back and edit, reorganize and prioritize your Mind Map.

To make Mind Mapping easier, a variety of software is available that allows it to be done on your computer screen. I've found this to be the most effective way for me to Mind Map. Doing it on the computer makes it extremely easy to add colors and graphics, group items, revise and edit your project. The software lets you link to urls, documents, and other Mind Maps. It also allows importing graphics, pictures, sounds and video clips that many find helpful. It's easy to make templates that can be modified for future use. (You *will* be writing and delivering a lot more speeches, won't you?)

On the opposite page is a graphic review of the above basics of Mind Mapping. (Remember to start in the middle of the page, then to 12:00, and go clockwise.)

For more information on Mind Mapping, and to see why it truly is "The *Swiss Army Knife* for the Brain!" go to http://mastermindmapper.com.

There's even an abbreviated Mind Map of the *No Sweat* Public Speaking! Formula here:
http://nosweatpublicspeaking.com/the-nsps-formula/

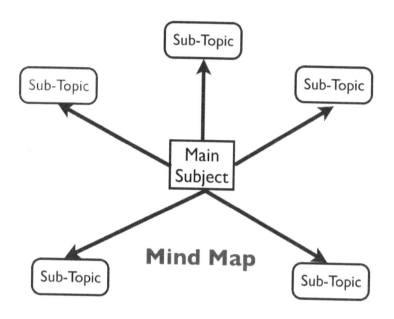

Graphics and Illustrations Help **GET IT!**

There are three communication styles: Visual, Auditory, and Kinesthetic.

Because people learn in different ways, the odds of the audience **Getting It!** increases as more of those methods of communication are used.

The book you're reading is visual.

My hope is that my writing also has a voice to it so you feel like you're hearing my message, one-on-one, from me to you.

To increase the odds of you getting my message, I've included illustrations, graphics, and Mind Maps.

The NSPS (*No Sweat* Public Speaking!) Mind Map starts at 12:00 o'clock and continues *clockwise*.

Opposite is a Mind Map of "How to Mind Map."

For additional information, go to http://mastermindmapper.com

There is a video that shows how to Mind Map here: www.mastermindmapper.com/Category/how-to-mind-map

Introduction –
No Sweat **Public Speaking!**

Picture this: It's ten o'clock Monday morning and your boss calls you into his office.

"Bill," he says. "As you know, this Friday is the most important day of the year for our company.

"It's our Annual Open House.

"One hundred of our top customers and fifty of the best prospects we've ever had will be here for the entire day.

"The president, CEO, and majority stockholder of the company requested that each department give a fifteen-minute presentation that day."

Your boss briefly looks down at what appears to be an agenda, looks up at you, and says, "I've got you scheduled to speak at 1:00, *right after lunch!*"

Now, there are three possible reactions to such an announcement.

THE FIRST ONE IS: "YES!"

"This is *my ticket* to the executive suite with a corner office, a key to the executive washroom, and my own parking spot!

"I am *always* ready to get up in front of an audience and *strut my stuff*!

"I can't wait for this opportunity!

"I am PUMPED! I wish it were this afternoon!"

A SECOND REACTION MIGHT BE: "PROZAC!"

"Me! Speak in front of a group! He's got to be kidding!

"This must be a bad joke. However, *I'm not laughing!*

"I still have nightmares about giving a book report in Mrs. Johnson's fifth grade classroom. It took me almost a half hour, with unscheduled bathroom breaks, to get through a five-minute presentation. I was so nervous that my legs start shaking every time I think about it."

"Giving presentations is <u>not</u> on my bucket list of things to do before I die!

"When I get off work, I'm heading to Walgreens and getting a triple refill. I'll start popping those puppies right at the druggist's counter.

"Friday Open House – I don't know whether I'll live that long!"

THE THIRD REACTION COULD BE: "COLONOSCOPY!"

"If this bozo thinks I'm going to put my whole career on the line in front of people I don't even know - he's nuts!

"When I get out of here, I'm going back to my office to call my gastroenterologist and reschedule that procedure for *this* Friday.

"Annual Open House – I'm out of here!"

Now, if your response to a request like this is closer to reactions two or three rather than number one – you are not alone!

Survey after survey has shown more people share the fear of speaking in public more than any other fear – including dying! Statistically, it affects as many as 75 percent of all people.

Jerry Seinfeld once said, "Most people, given the option at a funeral, would rather be in the box than give the eulogy!"

There's even a term for it – glossophobia – from the Greek glōssa, meaning tongue, and phobos, fear or dread.

A big part of the fear for most people speaking before a group is the belief that even if they survive the presentation, they'll do a lousy job, make a fool of themselves and damage their personal and professional reputations forever!

No wonder so many shy away from opportunities to speak!

This discussion reminds me of the time General Norman Schwarzkopf was in Saudi Arabia during Operation Desert Storm.

He was walking in the desert, contemplating the war, when

his foot struck something. The general reached down and picked up the object to see what it was. Upon closer examination, it appeared to be a bottle, covered with dirt and sand.

As he was brushing the grime off the bottle, lo and behold, a genie popped out and landed on the desert ground facing the general.

"General Schwarzkopf," he boldly announced, "*I* am the genie you've always heard about.

"*I* am the genie, Sir, who can grant you any request. Anything you want, Sir, ask me once and it shall *instantly* be yours."

The general didn't hesitate. He immediately reached into his back pocket and pulled out a long mailing tube. He pulled off the cap, reached in and pulled out a large piece of rolled up paper and proceeded to unroll that paper on the desert floor at the feet of the genie.

"This," he stated, "is a map of the Middle East. Since the beginning of time the people in this region have been fighting.

"I'm really glad you're here, Genie. My wish is that you *do your magic thing* and immediately stop forever the fighting in this area. After that, make it so these people will live forever, in peace and harmony, and help each other to survive and thrive.

"That's my wish, Genie. Go ahead and *do your thing!*"

The genie looked at the general, looked down at the bottle he had popped out of, and looked back at General Schwarzkopf.

"Sir, I told you I am the genie who can grant any wish. I have *never* failed.

"But, Sir, please take a look at this map. *These* people have been fighting since *before* the beginning of time!

"Think of all the broken peace accords and cease-fires that

didn't last a nanosecond!

"Now, I'm not saying you have to, but if you needed to come up with a second wish, what would it be, Sir?"

This sudden request caught the famous general off guard, but only for a moment.

"I've got it!" he exclaimed.

"With or without your help, Genie, this war will end someday. When it does, I'll be hanging up the uniform and retiring.

"My wife and I were discussing this just before my deployment and started to make plans for a second career when I pack it in and call it quits.

"We decided that I'm going to become a *professional speaker.* I don't mean just *a* speaker, but a real *professional* speaker. I want to be the *best* professional Public Speaker ever!

"I want the title of my presentation to always fill an auditorium to capacity.

"I want the Master of Ceremonies to give an introduction that gets people on their feet when I set a foot on stage and give me a standing ovation *before* I begin my talk.

"When I open my presentation, I want everyone on the edge of their seats, eagerly awaiting everything that follows.

"As I deliver the body of my talk, I want the audience attentive and nodding in the affirmative as I demonstrate the points of my message with great personal stories.

"When delivering my speech, I want all my verbal and nonverbal skills to be in perfect sync with my words and message.

"My eye contact, facial expressions, gestures, posture and body movements should be observed and felt by all in the room.

"My pronunciation and enunciation should be letter-perfect,

and everyone in the hall should be able to hear me clearly.

"I want to flawlessly use the other verbal communication skills of inflection, varying the cadence, and using pauses when appropriate.

"I don't ever want to use notes, and I don't want to leave anything out of my presentation.

"I always want to be composed and *never* experience stage fright or nervousness.

"I never want a prop to fail, a light not to work, or a sound system to sputter.

"When I tell a joke, I want the audience rolling in the aisles as if Leno and Letterman together had delivered the punch line.

"Finally, when I close my presentation, I want the entire audience to get to their feet, and with thunderous applause, give me another *standing ovation*!

"*That's* what I want, Genie! Go ahead, man, and do your thing!" exclaimed the General.

The Genie stood still. His face suddenly went pale.

He looked at the general, then he looked down at the bottle that he had popped out of, and then back at the general.

Finally, stuttering and stammering, he looked General Schwarzkopf in the eye and asked, "C-c-c-could I see that map *one more time,* Sir?"

Well, after relating this story, I've got *bad* news, and *good* news for you.

The **bad news:** There is no genie who's going to come along, snap his fingers, and make you a public speaker. (Trust me, if this dude existed, *I* would have found him by now.)

The *good* **news:** Public Speaking is a skill that can be *learned.*

Let me prove this to you.

Get hold of a small town newspaper (because they still do this) and look under Birth Announcements. You'll see boys are born and girls are born, but if your investigation is like mine, you won't see that any Public Speakers are born!

Now flip a few pages to the obituaries. (I never have understood how people die alphabetically!)

Read a few of the death notices and you'll find that people die from a variety of causes. I've yet to see where anyone died from giving a presentation!

This is great news!

We can deduce from this mini-investigation that there isn't a Public Speaking Gene you're either born or not born with.

We can also assume that giving a presentation is a relatively safe activity to engage in.

Therefore, we can conclude our research with this statement: "Somewhere between birth and death, Public Speaking is a skill that can be *learned!*"

You weren't born knowing how to do math, read, write, ride a bike, swim or any of the many other skills you possess, were you? Presentation skills are learned in the same manner: study, practice, and apply. Repeat that formula over and over and, like all your other skills, physical and mental, you'll improve!

In *No Sweat* Public Speaking!, I'll teach you the basics of developing, practicing, and delivering a presentation using the *No Sweat* Public Speaking! Formula. Sometimes, for brevity, I'll refer to it by its initials, NSPS.

I'll discuss the **Components, Parts,** and **Elements** of a good presentation. I'll name them, explain them, and give some examples along the way. We'll look at the Fear of Public Speaking and give suggestions for easing it. I'll also have Bonus Tips for Developing, Practicing, and Presenting your talk.

In the discussion will be a variety of valuable information on developing, practicing, and delivering *your* Knock Your Socks Off Presentation! – with *No Sweat!*

An important rule to always remember is that ALL the fundamentals of a presentation MUST be in sync. This is essential if the audience is going to receive and understand your core message. Remember, we want them to **GET IT!**

Getting It, as discussed in the Foreword to this book, is critical to all communication - verbal, written or visual.

Quickly as possible, we want the recipient(s) of our message to understand what we are trying to convey.

They may not agree with all of it.

They may not agree with *any* of it.

Until they **GET IT!** there cannot be a meaningful discussion going forward.

We're going to discuss a number of things that go into a good presentation. If they're not all delivering the *same* meaning, confusion will be the result. I'll have more on this later.

If you haven't already done so, please read the **Foreword** to learn why these graphics appear throughout the book.

They are part of the *No Sweat* Public Speaking! **Mind Map,** and directly relate to the subject and text. The complete Mind Map of the book is at www.nosweatpublicspeaking.com/book/mindmap

I used a Mind Map to write this book.

You'll find Mind Mapping to be an important and extremely useful tool for developing, practicing, and delivering a presentation.

For more information on Mind Mapping, and to see why it truly is "The *Swiss Army Knife* for the Brain!" go to http://mastermindmapper.com

Before Getting Started

For this book, the terms Public Speaking, Presentations, Speeches, Speaking, Giving Talks, etc. - consider them to be the same. Merriam-Webster may have a different opinion, and that's OK.

The reason I mention this stems from a conversation I once had with an ex-executive with Anheuser-Busch. I was telling him about my writings and talks on Public Speaking, and he said, "At Anheuser-Busch we never gave speeches or did public speaking, however, we delivered many Presentations."

That turned on a light bulb for me that I consider worth mentioning here.

Also, the book has been written and set up so readers can look at the Table of Contents and go directly to a chapter that gives the information they are seeking.

Some of what is found will also be in other sections of the book. Better to repeat than leave out crucial information that was mentioned previously, and didn't stick in the reader's mind. It also might be something they read later in the book. Again, better to reinforce than not.

Now, let's get started!

The Components, Parts & Elements of a Speech

There are two **components** to a presentation: **Content** and **Delivery.**

They must both be audience centered and in sync.

The **Content** of a presentation is your message. It's the information you want the audience to take away with them. It's the component of NSPS where your speech is developed. It might be something you've been assigned, or it could be a passion of yours that you chose.

The **Content** should consider your audience.

- What are their demographics?
- What is their experience with the subject you'll be presenting?
- Why are *they* in the audience?
- What are their current concerns and issues that your presentation addresses?
- What do you think they expect to take away from your talk?

It may be the twenty-ninth time you're going to present the same subject matter, but unless the above audience considerations are taken into account, and your message customized and tweaked to meet their expectations, don't expect anything but relief on their faces when you close your speech!

Regarding **Content**, always put yourself in the audience's shoes and ask: WIIFM - **What's In It For Me?**

They don't have to agree with your message, but they *do* have to understand it well enough to form an opinion. They have to **GET IT!**

Delivery is the presentation of that message to the audience; it literally *delivers* your content to the audience.

Most experts agree that **Delivery** is the most important component of a speech.

How your message is delivered is far more critical than *what* that message is. Now, this in no way negates the fact that **Content** must be relevant, informative, and valuable. It does point out the significance of a good presentation, and *again*, why *everything* must be delivering the *same* message.

The fact is this: You could be at the lectern and be very, very entertaining – and say nothing!

This is also true: You could be the foremost authority on a subject, but if you can't present to an audience in a manner that educates, entertains, and explains your knowledge, they won't **GET IT!**

The 2008 presidential race was won by Barack Obama, partly because of the extremely professional speaking skills he possesses. His orations took him to a rock star status in some people's minds.

He is not the only person to rise to this position with great presentation skills.

Ronald Reagan was called The Great Communicator.

Parts of John F. Kennedy's speeches are still quoted, and nearly everyone takes a second seat to Bill Clinton when it comes to delivering an address.

United States Presidents are not the only people we expect to be superb communicators. Our perception is that *Leaders* should be able to stand in front of an audience and make themselves understood in a professional and expressive manner.

Company leaders, Church leaders, Group leaders, School leaders, – and anyone in a leadership position, are expected to demonstrate some of that leadership ability speaking in front of others.

Some do. Many do not.

Because you're reading this book, you want to improve your communication skills. You either read, were told, or intuitively observed the value of being a good communicator.

This is a small book, but it's loaded with big ideas for accomplishing that goal.

Read it - Study it - Practice it.

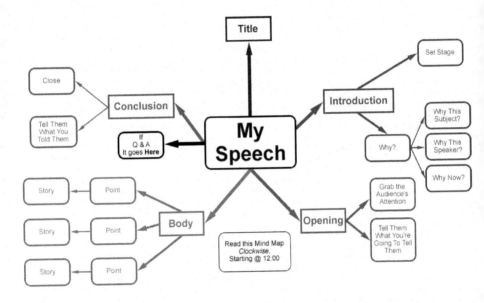

No Sweat Public Speaking!
Content Formula

The **NSPS Content Formula**, as noted below, can be used as a template for your speech:

- **Content**
  - » Title
  - » Introduction
  - » Opening
  - » Grab the audience's attention
  - » Tell them what you're going to tell them
  - » Body
  - » Tell them
  - » Conclusion
  - » Tell them what you told them
  - » Strong Closing

It can also be developed using the formula in a **Mind Map** format as shown on the opposite page. Additionally, it's available at: www.nosweatpublicspeaking.com/the-nsps-formula

Either way, the use of a template, made with word processing and/ or Mind Mapping software, can make developing your speech much easier than just sitting down and writing.

Because the templates break your task into modules, it's not as overwhelming as it first seems. (Like the same way you eat an elephant – one bite at a time!)

You'll be able to reuse several modules for many presentations, with little or no modification.

Before going through the modules, one by one, let's start in the middle of the Mind Map, or above the Title of the outline template. With as few words as possible, write **what your presentation will be about**. This will help mentally clarify that everything that follows is *in sync* with your main topic.

Consider the makeup of the audience when developing your talk: age, education, *why* they are in the audience, possible life experiences that relate to your speech, and *what* they expect to take away from your talk.

If you've ever taken a pubic speaking course or been a member of Toastmasters, you've heard the parts of a speech noted as: **Opening, Body,** and **Conclusion.**

These parts hold true, but they leave out, unfortunately, two very important parts: the **Title** and the **Introduction.**

Content

The Title

Think of the **Title** of your speech as if it was the title of a book, printed on its spine, and displayed on a shelf at Barnes & Noble.

When someone is eyeing the selection on the shelves in the section where they have an interest, *yours* should *jump out at them!*

The **Title** should jump out so much that the person takes the book from the shelf, reads the back cover, and opens it to read the front and back flaps.

After investigating the book (i.e., your speech) because the title grabbed their attention, they *buy* it; that is, they came to see you speak because they want to learn more!

Unless you absolutely must use a specific title, you may want to pencil in your first thought and finish it later. Remember, the title must be something that will make people want to come and see you speak.

The **Title of your Speech** is your newspaper headline, title on the spine of your book, and the words in the Subject Line of your most important email, all rolled up in one.

Just like the title of a new movie might get you to go online and look at the trailers, your speech title needs more consideration than many people think.

Editors know this: if the Headline of a newspaper article doesn't get your attention, you probably won't read the article. Also, an email with a Subject Line that doesn't immediately grab the recipient's attention might be deleted without being opened. The title to your talk should pull the audience in and make them want to know more.

Until Oprah quotes you on national television, a great title that draws people to your presentation wanting to know more, is your best chance at filling the auditorium.

Realistically, you might have been assigned or asked to do this talk by your boss or other official. Still, give it the thought it deserves. It may be after completing the development of your speech that the "Ah Ha!" title will come to you.

As an example, this book, and the signature speech I give by the same name, is *No Sweat* Public Speaking!

This title, I hope you agree, gets more attention than: *Presentations 101* or *How to Give a Good Presentation.*

You want the title to whet the appetite of the person who sees it; whet it enough for them to want to know more and see whether it's something they could benefit from.

You may even find it easier to write your speech first, and then come up with a title.

Have several titles in mind and bounce them off friends and family before deciding on one.

The same holds true for the **Subtitle** of your presentation. It explains more about the contents and goals of the speech, and is an integral and important part of the title. Don't neglect the power it can have!

Here, How to Develop, Practice, and Deliver a Knock Your Socks Off Presentation! with – *No Sweat!* reinforces the title message. It also adds enough information to entice people who might have thought the presentation and book was only about overcoming nervousness.

The Introduction

The **Introduction** to a speech is *not* the **Opening.**

The **Introduction** to a speech is also *not* your bio.

The **Introduction** is what the Master of Ceremonies presents to the audience *before* bringing you, the speaker, to the lectern.

The Introduction is an integral part of your speech. It is *extremely* important. Who is the person most qualified to write that important introduction? YOU!

Unfortunately, many speakers don't recognize this fact and give little, if any, attention to their introduction. Giving your Bio to the person introducing you, moments before your talk, does *not* address the importance of the Introduction. Do *not* downplay the impact an **Introduction** can have on the audience or how important it is to your entire presentation.

Just like the main attractions at many venues have *opening acts* that warm up the audience, the **Introduction** the Master of Ceremonies delivers warms up the audience to the point where *they've got to see the main event* – you!

THE THREE WHYS?

The Introduction should answer three questions:

Why this subject?

- Why the subject should be of interest to the particular audience it is being presented to. This should be customized, much as possible, for each audience.

Why this speaker?

- Why should this speaker - you - be talking about this subject? What specifically makes you qualified to present this topic? It might be experience, education, a passion for the particular subject, or a combination of things.

Why now?

- This part of the introduction should complete, in your audience's mind, why they are attending, why they should be attentive, and why they will benefit from your presentation.

Information that might be in your introduction:
- What is your education?
- What awards and recognitions have you received?
- What obstacles have you successfully overcome?
- What qualifies you to speak on this subject, to this audience, now?
- Why speak about it now?
- Where have you traveled, for what reasons and what did you see and learn?
- What have you built (i.e., business (es), nonprofit(s), inventions, community, family, etc.)?
- What research have you done on the subject.
- What articles and/or books have you written on the subject.
- Who have you spoken to before about this subject?

Some of the above, if relevant and appropriate to your presentation, should be in your introduction.

Also consider:
Who is your audience?
- What are their demographics and socioeconomic status? This should include: education, income, and occupation.
- What age range and ethnicity are you targeting? This information may affect the style you use to present your material.

Why are they attending?
- Is it a voluntary decision or mandate from their company, boss, partner, or someone else?
- Do they want to be there?

What is their investment to attend?
*   Time, money, or both?

What do they expect to learn from your talk?
*   *Are* they attending for pure entertainment or do they want something that will help get them closer to a personal or professional goal?

What do they already know about you and the topic you'll be speaking on?
*   It is to be hoped, the description of your presentation, before someone makes a decision to attend, should have been very specific about this. That description should serve as a filter for your audience.
    » Example: An experienced computer programmer would consider it a waste of time and money to attend a presentation geared towards educating computer novices on Basic Computer Skills.

The **Introduction** used for an audience of senior citizens might be considerably different from the introduction used for grade school children. (The speech will most likely be customized for those very different audiences, also.)

The **Introduction** sets the stage for your presentation and is an absolutely vital part of your speech. *You* should write the Introduction. Do it with the same mindset and tenacity used to develop and prepare your speech.

By *writing* the **Introduction**, I mean writing, rewriting, and rewriting, again. Yes, it's *that important!*

It's an opportunity to have someone else state your professional credentials and present evidence of legitimacy, or credibility.

It wouldn't be appropriate for you, the speaker, to go on and on about your degrees, honors, and accomplishments. It would be seen as boastful, and might even put a damper on the rest of your presentation. Much better this information be presented by the Master of Ceremonies, a third party, whose relaying of this information brings more credibility to the occasion.

This is *not* the time to be modest about your accomplishments.

- If you graduated at the top of your class, don't just say you were a graduate of such and such university.
- If you were in the top 10 percent of a national sales force of 235 people, don't write that you worked for XYZ company.
- If you worked your way through college waiting tables, and it has relevance to your credentials and speech – *write it*.
- If there is a particular obstacle you've overcome that is relevant to your presentation, this should be in the introduction, also.
- If your story were in the press, having the Master of Ceremonies hold up the article to show the audience will add to your credibility.

The **Introduction** should be like the king's trumpeters announcing that His Highness is on their way! It is *your* Hail to the Chief! and the red carpet is rolling out towards *you*.

Make it clear to the Master of Ceremonies that you will bring, or, better yet, send ahead of time, an **Introduction**.

Explain to the Master of Ceremonies that it is *an integral part of your presentation*. Tell them it's *your* responsibility to write it, and *their* responsibility to deliver it the way you wrote it. Be sure to review, and answer any questions they might have *before* the event.

A little role playing is a good idea here. Often, a *really* good idea! Master of Ceremonies are not all professional in their own presentations, and if not coached, could destroy your **Introduction**.

Since each **Introduction** should be tailored to the audience, *never* make the mistake of using a previous introduction without reviewing and editing. Use the basic template, but *customize* each one for time, place, audience and, often, the person introducing you!

A good **Introduction** is often delivered as if the Introducer wrote it. Prefacing an **Introduction** with words like, "Here's the Introduction Fred wrote for me to read," will sometimes diminish the effect of the words that follow. Point that out to the Master of Ceremonies!

Important: *Always* bring extra copies of your **Introduction** to the event. Even if you sent, reviewed, and confirmed the introduction with the Master of Ceremonies, *bring extra copies!* What if the person you arranged to make the introduction doesn't show up? What if he misplaced it?

Think of this as a *spare tire*. It is to be hoped that you never need it, but if you *have a flat*, this is the best remedy!

The last sentence of the **Introduction** should build the audience's excitement. The final words should be *your name*, and be spoken with an enthusiasm that starts the audience applauding. Example: "I'm excited, as I'm sure you are, to hear about planning a trip to Europe. Help me welcome _____ "

Following is the **Introduction** I use for my signature speech, *"No Sweat"* Public Speaking!

• • •

No Sweat
Public Speaking!
Fred E. Miller

Introduction Instructions

Read BOLD Words S-l-o-w-l-y
Emphasize and Pause briefly after each BOLD Word.
Thanks!

Our speaker today is a serial entrepreneur. His last enterprise was Business Research Bureau, a St. Louis sales lead subscription service.

Before owning Business Research Bureau he was in the **COFFEE SERVICE** business for many years.

Since he used to sell **COFFEE**, I asked him to **PERK UP** our meeting, and not let it become a **GRIND**.

Someone told me he **ESPRESSOS** himself well, and would *never* be considered a **DRIP**.

Many people find climbing the career ladder, or succeeding in one's own business, usually means doing some speaking in front of groups.

It's a credibility builder.

However, it's an activity *many* dread.

Even if you rarely speak in front of groups, the ability to do so greatly improves one-on-one communication and is a great confidence builder.

The fact is this: We *expect* our leaders to be great communicators and speakers.

If you *are* a leader or *want to be* recognized as a leader, our speaker today has a message for *you*.

He is a past president of his Toastmasters Club, where he was a member for many years.

He has spoken to local, regional and national groups.

I don't want to **SPILL THE BEANS** on his talk, and I'm eager, as I'm sure you are, to see what he's **BREWED UP** for us.

The title of his talk, and ***soon-to be-published book*** is: **No Sweat Public Speaking!**

Please help me welcome - Fred Miller!

● ● ●

The Master of Ceremonies then leads the audience in applauding as I rise and walk towards him. We shake hands, and he takes his place in the audience.

This **Introduction** gives some of my business background and speaking experience and adds a bit of humor with the *groaner* coffee language.

A few great things about an introduction like this:
- It gives the audience the information that answers the three *Whys?*
  - » *Why* this subject. *Why* this speaker. *Why* now?
- The humor relaxes the audience and piques their interest to hear from the man with the *groaner* Introduction. They know I'm not someone who takes myself too seriously.
- *Furthermore,* when I take the lectern, turn to the Master of Ceremonies, and say, "*Great* introduction, Bill! Thanks (pause) a *Latté!*" I get more positive laughter that puts *me* at ease!

Just as important as a good **Introduction** is the person delivering the Introduction and their delivery of your three *Whys?* This is why, and it bears repeating, it is *paramount* to review, *in detail,* your introduction with the person who will be delivering it.

If certain words should be emphasized in the delivery, highlight them in your text and be certain your Introducer knows how important, and what an integral part of the speech the introduction is. If he, or she, understands *their* importance in the emcee position, the results are bound to be better. Who knows, *they* may receive kudos for *their* part in the program!

I found out exactly how important this pre-event review is the hard way.

I had done a few morning mini-workshops at a manufacturing company, and it was time for a longer presentation in the afternoon with the entire company and their guests. I approached the Master of Ceremonies a few minutes before he took the stage and handed him my introduction.

He walked to stage center, glanced down and the paper I

had just given him, and said, "Our first presenter this afternoon doesn't need an introduction. We've already heard from him this morning. Come on up, Fred!"

I really had to back peddle and scramble my first few moments on stage because my plan had been to take off from the introduction I had written and jump right into my presentation.

A lesson learned!

On a *positive* note, at the sixtieth anniversary of my Toastmasters Club, the Master of Ceremonies did an *outstanding* job.

The president of the club called me a few months before the anniversary dinner and asked if I would speak. I replied that it would be an honor and asked who the other speakers would be.

"Paul and Sabine." was his reply.

"Yikes!" I said to myself. They are both friends and excellent presenters. Paul is an attorney, a council member in his city, and an eloquent speaker. Sabine is an author who speaks professionally all over the country. She delivers *great* presentations. I did *not* want to follow those two speakers. Maybe you've been in the position of speaking after someone who is *really, really* good. I've been there, and it is not fun.

"OK," I said, "but I'd like to speak first."

"Sorry, Fred," was the reply. "I've already talked to each of them. You're my third call and you're batting *cleanup*. See you at the event!"

Bummer! I knew I needed a plan, and decided to make my Introduction part of it. I would write an Introduction that would take the attention *off* the previous speakers and *on* to me.

I used the above **Coffee** Introduction, but knew I had to add something to accomplish my goal. Because I was the last speaker of the evening, and following Paul and Sabine, I wrote the following, to be read by the Master of Ceremonies, to precede it:

"As promised, we've had two *great* speeches this evening. Paul and Sabine are absolutely two of the best speakers this club has ever produced. Let's have another round of applause for both of them." David, the emcee that evening, then lead the attendees in applause.

He continued, "If you've read the program, you've noticed that there's one more speaker this evening. I'm sure you're all familiar with the expression, "We've saved the best 'til last! (pause) Well, (long pause) *maybe not tonight!*"

David did it *so well* everyone thought the line was *his*. The audience loved this and burst out laughing as they all looked at me for a reaction.

I played along with the scenario and gave them an expression indicating, "I can't believe he said that!"

David continued introducing me using my *Coffee Groaner* script. That combination Intro truly got my speech off to a great start and the entire presentation went well.

The Opening

After the **Introduction**, you begin your speech with the **Opening**.

The **Opening** serves two purposes:
- Grabs the audience's attention.
- Tells them what the speech will be about.

GRAB THEIR ATTENTION

If you capture your audience's attention from the get-go, it will be easier to keep it as you continue your talk. They'll *want* to hear what you have to say. If they *want* to hear you speak, it's more likely they'll **GET IT!**

The **Opening** of your speech is often *the audience's first impression of you*. It should be strong. It will be one of the first things the audience remembers when reflecting upon your presentation.

It sets the stage for everything that follows.

Very quickly, the audience will be on the edge of their seat, either breathlessly waiting for more, or, if your opening isn't a great one, waiting for the moment they can leave their seat and bolt for the exit!

The opening should *not* be a perfunctory, "Thank you for inviting me," or "I'm privileged to address you this evening," or, "It is great to be back at _____."

Think of the **Opening** of your speech as the headline of a newspaper article.

If the article grabs the attention of the reader, they'll read further.

If the audience likes your **Opening,** they'll want to hear more. They will be paying attention.

There's only one chance to make a first impression – and this is it!

Your goal here is to connect and engage your audience.

The **Opening** should be strong, and there are a number of ways to ensure that it is:

1. Open with a question.

Examples:

- "What would you do if, when hearing the latest Powerball Lottery numbers announced, you suddenly realized *you* had matched *all* six?"
- "Where were *you* on 9/11 and how did you first hear about the attack?"

A tip about asking questions: When *you* raise *your* hand while asking, there will be a larger response than if your hand remains by your side. Increasing audience participation is a *good thing* when giving a speech!

Another tip: After asking a question pause for a moment to allow the question to sink in a bit. This allows the audience time to start processing the question. Do this for a rhetorical question, also.

2. Present a famous quote.

Example:

• One of my favorite Abraham Lincoln quotes is: "Things may come to those who wait...but only the things left by those who hustle."

• You could then follow with, "Let me tell you about someone who *hustles*. . . ."

Quoting from well-known people lets you tap into *their* message, credibility, and history.

3. Start with a story or anecdote.

People love stories. I'm sure you've heard them as a child at bed-time, and told them as an adult. You, like me, can also remember sitting on the floor and listening to a teacher read a great story.

Do your best to make this a *personal* story. Usually, this will mean it will be something they haven't heard before versus the tried and true stories of others that get told over and over.

Example:
- "I remember sitting on the bus at Fort Bragg, North Carolina. It seemed like one of the lowest points of my life – waiting to start Army Basic Training. Suddenly, the silence was broken by someone shouting my name. I looked up and saw Barry, a good friend of mine from high school!"

4. If you have a special talent, you might use it in your **Opening**, but only when it is relevant to your speech. For instance, if you can perform magic, you could start with a trick. Maybe one of your magic tricks is making money disappear, and your talk is about the changing economy and what people can do to keep up with the changes.

Perhaps you play an instrument. You might play a song. Here, again, this must be relevant to your theme. A funeral dirge and the benefits of planning and prepaying your own funeral could fit with your speech on the economy.

5. Use a Visual.

A visual could be a prop, a picture, or *you*! Yes, *you* could come center stage, dressed as a symbol that has something to do with the core message of your speech.

Example:
- If you are speaking about the problems of the homeless, your *costume* might include wearing old clothes and carrying a garbage bag filled with your life's possessions.

6. Make a declarative statement or give an alarming statistic.

Let's say you're giving a speech about prostate cancer. Your **Open-**

ing declarative sentence could be, "It is estimated that 186,320 men will be diagnosed with and 28,660 men will die of cancer of the prostate this year." This could be followed by, "Let me see the hands, please, of all the men who regularly get checked for this treatable disease."

7. Paint a word picture.

No physical pictures equal what our minds can develop. Use words like, "Picture this" or "Just for a moment, imagine your-self..." We think in terms of pictures, so this **Opening** technique can be particularly effective.

Example:

- "Picture this. You've just taken your seat in English Class, and the professor says, "Class, clear your desks and take out a clean sheet of paper and pen." What are your thoughts?

8. Suspense/Surprise

Build suspense with the audience. Then, surprise them with a *contrary* statement.

Example:

- "In preparing for this presentation over a period of two weeks time, I took over 200 pictures. I then picked the 15 best ones, cropped and edited them to get the exact content I needed to make my points today, loaded them into a PowerPoint presentation - and then my hard drive promptly crashed!"

9. Use something timely in your Opening.

The use of recent material refreshes your introduction and shows the audience that you're on top of your subject.

A current event, if appropriate, can be used very effectively in an opening. If it's print media you're using, that item can also be used as a prop, and held up as you speak your opening words.

Example:

- "I noticed in this morning's paper there was another shooting in the city – and the victim was only 14 years old! *When, when, when* – are we going to seriously address the handgun issue in this country?"

10. Do something unusual.

Example:

- I have a friend who told me the story of how she got into business for herself. It was the stress of the job she was in at the time, plus putting in far too many hours. She woke up in a hospital with tubes attached to her and the sound of the heart monitor that was next to her bed.

The suggestion for Opening her presentation I made was to shake the hand of the Master of Ceremonies, walk to the lectern, pause, and hit the play button of a recorder. Immediately, the audience would hear: Beep - Beep - Beep - Beep - Beep - Beep - Beep - Beep - Beep.

After 30 seconds of this she was to address the audience and say, "Who knows that sound? (Pause) What is it?

After someone answers, "Heart monitor," she could continue, "Right! (Pause) Picture this - It was . . . " and start her personal story.

Here are some **Additional tips for your Opening** that also relate to your total speech:

Use *vivid* words.

The more senses you involve and the more explicit the details you use in your presentation, the more attentive and involved your audience will be. Describing the taste, smell, and feel of something rather than just naming an object, makes the speech come alive for the audience.

- **Example:** You *don't* suddenly "feel like having a slice of pie."
  - » You *do* tell the audience about being in your bedroom, upstairs and "smelling apple pie as it bubbles over the homemade crust and onto the hot cooking sheet. Then you begin to salivate as you think about a scoop of ice-cold, Breyer's French Vanilla Ice Cream melting on a huge slice. In your mind's eye you see the ice cream transforming into a liquid as it settles onto the warm pie. You race down the steps toward the kitchen even *before* being asked whether you're hungry!"

Don't start talking immediately when you're introduced.
Pause – and count silently to five.
- The silence signals the audience to stop, look, listen, and give you their undivided attention.

Smile before speaking
Unless your presentation is a somber one, smiling indicates you are confident, and ready to present!

Never, even if true, tell the audience you are unprepared for your presentation.

Statements like that are self-destructive. The audience will not expect much from you, and you'll probably meet their low expectations.

If there's humor in your opening, and it's appropriate, and you can present it well – use it!

Good humor will put the audience, and you, at ease.

TELL THEM WHAT YOU'RE GOING TO TELL THEM

Your audience wants to know what's next.

The program agenda, your introduction and opening all gave them an idea of what they'll be hearing.

This part of the **Opening** tells them what will follow. It's important because it will confirm that they are in the right place to learn something they have an interest in.

It's also the place where you will tell them the structure of your talk and how you will handle questions they might have.

The audience wants to know where they are going and how they will get there.

If you were on a cross-country trip, and needed to reach your destination quickly, would it make sense to leave the highway and take roads that lead in different directions? Consider your presentation in the same, "Direct from here to there" manner. This may take some editing and reworking, but you don't want the audience to wonder, "What has *this* got to do with the theme?" or

"Why is he telling us *that?*"

Example: This is one of the **Tell Them What You're Going to Tell Them** elements of the **Opening** *I* use.

"I'll be presenting the Components, Parts, and Elements of *No Sweat* Public Speaking!
I'll *name* them, *explain* them, and give some examples.
Next I'll talk about the Fear of Public Speaking, and give some suggestions for easing it.
I'll give you some Bonus Tips for Developing, Practicing, and Presenting your talk.
Next we'll have some time for your Questions.
Finally, I'll conclude my presentation.
Let's get started!"

Please review the above. It's important, and often left out by speakers who should know better.

It's a very succinct and explicit roadmap that tells the audience exactly what they can expect from me. They know what, and when, I will cover particular things.

They are also told *specifically* when questions will be taken. Telling them in this manner lessens hands being raised and/or questions being shouted during my presentation.

The Body

Now it's time to "**tell them what you're going to tell them.**"

This is the main part of your message. This is the meat of your **Content**.

Here, I'll be continuing my discussion of the **Components, Parts,** and **Elements** of the *No Sweat* Public Speaking! Formula.

As mentioned, *everything* about your presentation should be in sync. *Everything* should support the main theme.

Again, there should be only *one* main theme. *Everything* in your speech should support that one main theme.

In the **Body**, there should be *three to five points* that support the main theme.

There's a widely accepted formula for the **Body** that goes like this:

Make a point – tell a story.
Make a point – tell a story.
Make a point – tell a story.

All the stories should support the individual points, and all the points should support the theme. (Technical Presentations may not follow this formula, but could often benefit by utilizing parts of it.)

For instance, when I speak about the **3 Ps of Selling**, *selling* is my main theme.

I then name the **3 Ps: P**roduct Knowledge, **P**rospecting, and **P**ersistence.

As each point is named and explained, I tell a story that supports the point.

The important thing about the story is that it should be *personal –your* story! This isn't always possible to do, but, as you'll see in the following example, there are good reasons to use your own experience to prove a point.

For example, when I talk about **P**ersistence in Selling, I emphasize how vital persistence is to the sales process.

I tell the audience that selling is a *process*, not an event. I let them know them that I attended a seminar once that mentioned a survey that found most sales take twelve touches (phone call, email, postcard, etc.) to close, and that most salespeople bail after only four tries.

The next thing I do is to tell a story to support "Persistence in Selling."

I talk about Thomas Edison, one of the greatest inventors of all time - a true genius.

The Persistence Story about Edison is that it took him 10,000 tries to invent the light bulb.

A reporter asked him, "How does it feel to have failed 9,999 times?"

Edison's reply was, "I never failed! I successfully discovered 9,999 ways *not* to make a light bulb. Each experiment got me closer to the result - a light bulb!"

Now, all tales tend to grow through the years, and it might not have been 10,000 times.

However, using Thomas Edison and this story of not giving up and persevering until the desired goal is obtained, is a great illustration of the lesson is that *it pays to be persistent.*

Persistence can change the future of the world!

The problem with *this* story, and many others, is that *many* people have already heard it - perhaps you!

I once attended a seminar where I heard that story - *twice*! One speaker, obviously not listening to the one who preceded him at the lectern, told the *same* Edison light bulb story!

The answer to this problem is simple: **Tell *your own* story!**

It's important to the success of your presentation: **Tell your own story!**

As an example, here is **my persistence story:**

I was in the Coffee Service business for many years.

At one point, we started handling a coffee system that would brew a single cup at a time. *Not* instant coffee, but real *fresh-brewed* coffee. The coffee and the filter were in a single capsule-like container.

Besides making a cup at a time, there were many coffee choices: regular, decaf, flavored and different blends.

The whole system offered *many* advantages: no waste, very little time in preparation or cleaning, choices for all tastes, etc. It truly was a revolutionary idea for the Coffee Service industry.

In the cross hairs of my sales target was a locally owned chain of banks.

I knew they had a Coffee Bar in their lobby where clients and employees could go for a cup of Joe. This meant they were a high-volume user and put them high on my prospect list.

It was an upscale bank, so I figured our new gourmet, single-cup, fresh-brew system would be a perfect fit for them.

A good selling tactic is to start at the top with Vito – the Very Important Top Officer.

With this in mind, I called the chairman of the board ... and I *called* the chairman of the board ... and I *continued* to call the chairman of the board. I called *repeatedly*; no luck getting through to him.

Then one day I saw an article in the paper featuring him and the fact that he collected circus memorabilia.

Thinking this might be an attention-getter for securing an appointment, I sent him a copy of the article with a note stating, "Richard, I saw this and thought you might want another copy.

"By the way, I've seen your Coffee Bar. If you ever want to upgrade it, I have something that might be a fit."

I followed that note up with a phone call, another phone call, and several additional calls before finally getting Richard on the phone. (This *is* my Persistence Story, isn't it?)

When we spoke, he mentioned a coffee brewing system he enjoyed at one of the airline clubs at the airport and said he might consider switching to it.

I said, "Richard, I'm familiar with that machine. It's an excellent choice, but it doesn't offer the variety that the system I'm suggesting does. Additionally, ours is *much* easier to clean and maintain.

"By the way, do you drink coffee, Richard?"

"I *love* a good cup of coffee," he replied.

I went on to close the appointment and asked, "What would fit your schedule better - Tuesday or Wednesday next week?"

He replied, "Tuesday," and we set the time for 2:00 PM.

Before hanging up, I exclaimed, "Richard, *wait till you taste the French Roast!*"

On the day of the appointment I was early, and thoroughly prepared.

I got into the elevator that led to the Executive Office Suite. I was ready for anything. My goal was to perform a demonstration.

For this sales call, being prepared meant using my dolly to carry a coffee brewer, water bottle, pump, many coffee samples, signage, and everything else needed for a demo.

I was led into Richard's office promptly at 2:00.

We exchanged a few pleasantries, and he noted that he liked aggressive salespeople. ("Good!" I said to myself.)

About that time, a gentleman wearing a suit walked into the room, handed Richard some papers, and glanced at me.

Richard introduced me to Ken, the president of the bank, and told him why I was visiting.

We shook hands, and Ken promptly left the office.

Richard and I had barely begun to talk again when the phone on Richard's beautiful walnut desk rang.

Richard answered - it was Ken! Because it was a small room, and Ken's voice was loud on the other end, I could hear the conversation!

"What in the world are you doing talking to this guy, Richard?" I heard Ken ask.

"Not only is our present coffee supplier a *customer* of the bank, he's a *friend of yours!*

"Get rid of him. We've got work to do!"

I heard a click on the other end of the phone, and watched Richard put his handset into its cradle.

He looked up from the desk and stared straight at me.

"We're going to have a problem with Ken," he stated.

I had come too far to give up, so I asked, "You once told me you like coffee, didn't you Richard?" I asked.

"Yes, but . . ." he started to say.

Jumping to my feet, I interrupted him and exclaimed, *"Wait till you taste the French Roast!"*

Without looking at Richard for approval, I grabbed my dolly with all its coffee supplies and headed out of his office and towards the elevator.

A flying tackle would have been the only way to stop me.

"Come down in about 45 minutes and try the coffee!" I shouted as the elevator door closed behind me.

When the doors opened on the ground floor, where the coffee bar was, I didn't waste any time getting my demo set up.

Sure enough, about 45 minutes later, Richard came down to try a cup of fresh-brewed French Roast Coffee.

I handed him a K-Cup (a small container holding a filter and enough coffee to make a fresh brewed cup of coffee in just moments).

He placed the K-Cup in its designated spot, put his coffee cup where indicated, and, as I instructed, pushed the start button.

Very quickly, he had a full cup of coffee and the system was ready for its next customer.

He liked it, and seemed to approve when I started showing customers and employees how to use the machine and make a single cup of *fresh-brewed* coffee.

With the coffee bar filled with people making and drinking coffee I turned to Richard and said, "How about this, Richard? I'll come in tomorrow morning, bring lots of supplies, and treat your employees, and customers to my products. Then you can poll them and determine if my system would be a fit for the bank. *No charge* - it's all on me!"

Richard agreed to the *Free Test Drive*, and we shook hands.

The following morning I was at the bank early.

I set up everything and started buttonholing people to show them how to brew their own cup of java.

Things were going really well - many folks getting their own coffee, both bank customers and employees.

Then, at 9:00, Ken walked into the bank. He took one look at what was going on, immediately walked up to me, got right up into my face and said, "What are YOU doing here!"

I answered, "Well, I talked to Richard after we did a little coffee tasting yesterday and offered to come in this morning and do the same thing for all your employees and customers. We could then poll everyone to see whether it might be something worth bringing into the bank."

Ken pointed his index finger directly at me and declared, "YOU were supposed to talk to ME!

"MY office - 15 minutes!"

If you have ever been in sales, you'll quickly note that Ken's remarks and body language were *not* buying signals!

Promptly at 9:25, as *suggested* by Ken, I walked into his office.

The only thing I could think to do was immediately *fall on the sword.*

"I apologize, Ken," I said when I walked into his office.

"*Completely* my fault!" I went on.

"Obviously, I misunderstood something last night. I take full responsibility for setting up the coffee tasting without first consulting you."

Figuring these statements would throw some *cool* water on his *hot* temper; I sat down in the chair he motioned me to sit in.

Wrong!

When I started getting comfortable, he declared, "That doesn't even matter!

"I've talked to some of my people who tried your coffee. *Nobody* had anything great to say about it. Several commented how hot it was. Statements like that get me very concerned that a customer could burn themselves, and we'd get sued!"

I'd worked too long and come too far to give up now. (Remember, this is *my* Persistence Story!)

The only thing I thought would save me from getting kicked out of the bank immediately was to ask a question. There was only one question that made sense to ask.

So I asked Ken, very nicely, "Are *you* a coffee drinker?"

That *really* caught him off guard.

Stunned by the question, he answered, "Well, sure. I drink about five cups a day."

Now, there was only one thing I could do and say. I rose to my feet and started towards the door of his office, and exclaimed, "*Wait till you taste the French Roast!*"

He would have had to call Security to stop me.

When the dust settled, I installed a coffee brewing system in the coffee bar area and one in the employee lounge.

I also persuaded Ken to replace their bottled water service with one of our filtered water systems. "Better water makes better coffee!" I told him.

It was not long after this installation my company was asked to do the same at all the bank's branch locations.

Now, that's *my* Persistence Story.

No one else can tell *that* story!

Anyone can tell, and many *have* told, the Thomas Edison Persistence Story.

The point is this, and it's extremely important to the body of your speech: *Each of us* has a *personal* story to tell.

You have stories of: overcoming adversity, not quitting, speaking your mind when it wasn't the popular belief, and other stories from *your* school of hard knocks.

Here's the Key to this part of *No* Sweat Public Speaking! Do as they say in practicing yoga – "*Be present* on the journey and *always in the moment.*"

Be aware of *what's* happening *when* it's happening.

Then, when those stories occur in real time, *capture* them, and put them in the hard drive that is your brain!

Do this, and you'll start building files of stories to use when you're developing and preparing a speech.

Then use these in the *Make a Point - Tell a Story* elements part of the body of your talk.

Additional Tip: When capturing those stories in real time, capture as *much detail* as possible

Use your senses to catch the moment, and replay, with all the detail, to the audience when making your point. (It doesn't hurt to have a digital recorder handy for detailing the specifics of stories you want to file in your brain for future speeches.)

Example: It wasn't a *winter* night.

It was a *bone chilling, pitch dark, winter* night that no one with any sense of well-being should have been out in. Yet, there I stood, over an *ice-coated grate* in the street, trying to think *warm* thoughts, and hoping nothing dire had delayed her arrival.

Do this:
Start a file, or better yet, files, for future presentations. Make headings such as: Honesty, Overcoming Adversity, Helping Others, Being Helped by Others, Persistence, etc.

Then fill those files with personal stories while they're fresh in your mind, including all the specifics you can think of while they're crisp. You'll soon build up a reservoir of great material to help make your points in future presentations.

Telling **the story** is only an expression.

When appropriate, *Act Out* your story. Bring it to life in the minds of your audience.

Use imagery and theatre in your presentation. Perform so well that they feel they are in the story you're relating. When people emotionally *feel* what you're telling them, your presentation goes to an entirely different level.

We think in terms of pictures and associations. Use vivid descriptions to get into the minds of your audience and communicate on an emotional level.

For some of the *Best* information on story telling, go to Doug Stevenson's site, www.storytelling-in-business.com. Doug is the *master* of this technique. Search for him on YouTube.com and view a master practicing his craft.

YOUR CONTENT

Obviously, before developing your talk, you need to have a subject to speak about.

Sometimes, this will be a no-brainer, because it would have been assigned to you.

In Toastmasters, we are asked to do a series of speeches based on different aspects of speaking. The first one is the Icebreaker Speech, where the speaker tells the membership something about him or herself. Others include: Vocal Variety, Show What You Mean, Persuade with Power, and similar speeches that have the member emphasize a specific skill. *You* pick the subject.

If the topic is *your* decision, the easiest thing is to start on a subject you know a lot about and have a passion for. This could be job related, a hobby, a personal passion, or experience, or a charitable cause you support.

The subject matter could be extremely personal and best for a limited audience with similar challenges, or it could be something universal that almost anyone would have an interest in learning about.

Keep in mind the **3 E's of Public Speaking: Educate – Entertain – Explain.**

- **Educate** the audience about your subject so they take away knowledge about it they might not have had before your talk. You want them leaving the venue with more information than they arrived with.
- **Entertain** them!
  - » Entertained people are more attentive. When they are

attentive, the odds of them **Getting It!** increase. We like to be entertained!

- **Explain** your message.
  - » Be certain that as you entertain them, you are explaining in a manner that can be understood by most of the attendees.
  - » The less they have to work to understand your message, the more likely they will be receptive to it. If it's a lot of work to understand what you're trying to convey, you'll lose your audience.
  - » People have different learning styles: Auditory, Visual, and Kinesthetic. Try to have your presentation address each of them.

The best route for many is to pick a subject, *then* seek out specific audiences where their speech will be a fit.

Use a Mind Map to brainstorm many subjects. Prioritize them according to topics you have the most interest in and think have the widest appeal. Go back to this Mind Map several times to review and revise. This process will help you hone in on topics to work on speeches now, and later.

One of the main considerations will be: *Who* is the audience and *what* is their knowledge and interest in your topic? With few exceptions, especially with your initial speaking goals, there's no sense talking to an audience that sees no value in your subject matter. Why start with an audience that doesn't care or could be hostile to your subject matter?

Find those groups, seeking your specific topic and start speaking and honing your skills. Every time you give a presentation it will be a learning experience. You'll learn what information you *should* have included, and what information to leave out the next time.

Though you know your subject matter, continue to research it and refresh your material. This exercise will hone your investigatory skills. It's an opportunity to grow. You'll learn new things and have an opportunity to increase your presentation skills.

The internet makes it easy to find out the latest on any topic. Even it you speak about an old topic; there might be new information available.

Often, I thought I had all the relevant information at hand, but decided to Google one more time. The result was sometimes a rewrite of a portion of my talk.

Finding the latest on your subject matter also goes a long way toward the expert perception we spoke of earlier. Not doing this can have the opposite effect.

Expand your interests and you'll expand your inventory of subjects to speak about. Be curious. If you see, read, or hear something that grabs your attention – investigate it a bit further. It may turn out to be something new, exciting, and something to build a presentation around.

There are also great speech writers and researchers who can help you with content.

Example

I never did many PowerPoint/Keynote Presentations. I forced myself to do this when I told a group I would present to that I didn't have a projector. Someone quickly volunteered theirs. Yikes!

I then dived into studying the best practices of slides. I read articles by Guy Kawasaki and the book, Presentation Zen, by Garr Reynolds. The subject, How to Use Slides in a Presentation, is now an integral part of my talks, and extremely relevant to *No Sweat Public Speaking!*

The important thing is not *how* you get started, but to *get started!* Get something down on paper. Keyboard your thoughts into a word processing program or into the section of a Mind Map.

If you don't use the NSPS Speaker's Template, use the *No Sweat Public Speaking!* Content Formula outline shown earlier in the book, and start filling in the different sections.

Some people would rather dictate than write. That's fine. Record your thoughts, then either transcribe them, or job it out. There are plenty of places you can send a wave file to, and they'll quickly send you a word file.

Once you see something beginning, you'll be motivated to add, revise, and edit your talk. You're on your way!

Hint
Carry a digital recorder. When something catches your attention or you suddenly think of a subject that might be future speaking material – record the thoughts. You can then put them into a Speech Subject File. Periodically review this and start building your repertoire of expertise and presentation subjects.

Keep it *Simple*
- It might be a complex topic, but simplify it.
- *Simple* doesn't mean dumb down or stupid. *Simple* means the audience **GETS IT!** They don't have to think hard and try to

figure out the meaning of everything you say.

- Discard extraneous phrases, tech jargon and anything else that could cause the audience to scratch their heads in confusion.
- As you develop your material, continually put yourself in the future audience and ask, "So what?" "What has *that* got to do with this subject?" and "What does that mean to *me?*"

Keep in Mind

- Good writing is *specific writing.*
- Good *speaking* contains *specifics.*

Language

Check the words you use for anything that might offend.

- Words that are sexist, smack of racism, put down someone's ethnicity, religion, physical attributes, sexual orientation, or profane, are unacceptable. They will quickly turn off an audience.

Use proper English.

- It needn't be prim and proper, but it does have to be correct. Saying, "Bob and me is going to the ball game," is like chalk scratching on a blackboard for many people. Spout several phrases like that and you'll quickly lose your credibility and audience.

Keep Focused - Use this Content Exercise

When my audience reflects on my presentation, they will remember:

1. _____

2. _____

3. _____

The Conclusion

The final part of a speech is the **Conclusion**.

The **Conclusion** has two elements.

The **Summary** and the **Closing**.

First, we *"tell the audience what we told them."*

Second, we *close the speech.*

If we make a decision to include time for a **Question and Answer Session**, this *must* be done *before* the Conclusion. I'll have more on this later, but it's important that Q&A, if part of your presentation, is *not* the conclusion of your talk. The **Closing** part of the Conclusion is the Closing – Period!

SUMMARY

Let's discuss the *Tell Them What We Told Them* aspect, the **Summary** element of your closing. It's somewhat the mirror image of the Opening where you *Told Them What You Were Going to Tell Them*.

We do this to reinforce our message, and bring it together.

A good technique for helping people recall and understand the points you've made is **Repetition**: Repeat, repeat, and repeat, your message.

The more we hear, see, and are exposed to something, the better our recall and understanding. This is one way to insure our audience **Gets It!**

Have you ever read a book or article or seen a movie more than once and received information you didn't get the first time? Sure! That's human nature and normal. Our attention span usually isn't exceptionally long. It's natural, even if your presentation is a great one, that everyone will not receive and understand your complete message the first time it's presented. (I've repeated a number of things in this book for that exact reason. I want *you* to **GET IT!**)

Now, I'm not saying to repeat your speech word-for-word, but do give a summary of the main points.

Tell the audience what you're going to do.

Example: "Before I close my talk, let's review what we've discussed today . . ."

Hit those highlights in your **Conclusion**, sometimes assigning numbers to them, and perhaps using different language than first used. Whether the audience agrees with you or not, at least they're more likely to understand and remember what you said than if you didn't remind them in the summary element of your conclusion.

One of our goals, remember, is that the receivers of your message **GET IT!** They may agree with all, some, or none of it. What's important here is when you close your presentation, they should completely *understand* the points of your talk. If they don't understand the content of your message, *they'll* consider their time wasted, and *you* won't achieve the goals you set.

THE CLOSING

Finally - the **Closing!**

Before closing, *tell* the audience you are about to close the speech. This is *important*. It's OK if your closing has a surprise in it, but *not* if your closing *is* the surprise!

I've attended presentations, as I'm sure you have, where the speaker suddenly stopped talking. The audience didn't know whether he had lost his thoughts, forgot the next part of his presentation, was pausing for effect, had sudden heartburn, or finished speaking. Closings like these sometimes become anti-climatic endings to otherwise fine presentations. *Don't* do this to *your* audience!

Have you ever been enjoying a movie and all of a sudden, when you weren't expecting it, there's an *underwhelming* ending and the credits start rolling? Your thoughts are that you've missed something and possibly wasted your time, right?

Don't cheat *your* audience!

Here's another analogy. You're on a trip and have been leisurely driving down the road for a while. There's a large, wide bend in the road and as you drive it and the road starts to straighten out, suddenly, and with no signs to warn you, *there's a dead end!*

Don't do that to your audience. Give them the sign that it's time to close the speech. They'll appreciate it. Everyone wants to know the itinerary of the trip, *don't they?*

Here are some ways to tell them:
- "It's time to conclude this presentation."
- "I'm going to close my presentation with a . . ."
- "Let me close my talk by . . ."
- "My watch says it's time to close. So, . . ."

People will remember the first and last things they hear from you. We call this "The Law of Primacy and Recency."

This is why it is *mandatory* that you have a **strong opening** and a **strong closing**. Of the two, more often than not, the **closing** will be recalled more than any other part of the presentation.

This bears repeating: When your audience is reflecting upon your talk, the *last* thing you say will probably be the *first* thing they will remember.

Memorize and practice, practice, practice your opening and closing! Rehearse it so it becomes second nature to you.

Remember, though, it's the first time *this* audience will hear it. Don't lose the enthusiasm and emotion you had when delivering the closing many audiences ago!

Consider:
Courtroom summations by attorneys will likely be the words most remembered by jurors as they head to deliberating a verdict.

In **political debates**, the closing statements of the candidates can, and often do, carry a disproportionate amount of influence to voters than most of what took place in the debates. The candidate with the last closing statement also has a bit of an advantage over his or her opponent(s).

For these reasons, your **Closing** must be strong and compelling. You're going for a *Knock Out!* It is what the audience will probably remember most, and it's certainly your final opportunity to make a lasting impression.

You want the audience exclaiming, "Yes!" and "Wow!" while rising to their feet in a thunder of applause!

Saying, "Thank you!" to an audience is *not* a closing, and certainly not memorable. It lets them down. They feel cheated. This is especially true if your presentation was good. You've heard speakers close like that, haven't you? It's terrible!

When your presentation is concluded and you've done your job correctly, the audience will be thanking *you!*

Your **Closing** can take several forms, and should always be relevant to your talk.

Possible Forms

Call to Action
- Ask your audience to do something.
- **Example:** John F. Kennedy began the closing of his inaugural speech with, "And so, my fellow Americans: ask not what your country can do for you - ask what you can do for your country."

Challenge
- If you've been speaking on physical fitness and state that the importance of exercise is losing weight and lowering

cholesterol, say, "Right here, right now – *Everyone* who thinks following the 5 *Steps to a Better YOU Program* could make major changes in your health and self-esteem - get on your feet – raise your right hand - and repeat after me, 'I ...."

Humor

- If you have used Humor during your speech, and if it's appropriate to the message and audience, using humor to close can work well. People like to feel good, correct? If your presentation leaves them smiling and laughing, that's a good thing!

Quotation or Story

- If, on the other hand, the message was serious and thought-provoking, a closing that ends with a **Quotation** or **Pulling-at-the heartstrings story** that succinctly summarizes your message, will be very effective.

- **Example:** "Steve Jobs would not have continued to lead Apple had it not been for the generosity of a family who lost a loved one in an auto accident. If you haven't signed an organ donor card, I hope you'll now consider *the gift of life.*"

Switching Delivery Styles

- A quiet, solemn closing, in contrast to a speech that was high-energy and full of humor, will be the kind of *pattern interrupt* that will have the most effect on the audience as you leave the lectern. Since this is not the closing they were expecting it will leave the them thinking hard about your message.

- **Example:** "We've had fun today talking about ways to conserve energy and alternative sources of energy. These are subjects many of us, get energized just thinking about. That's great!

- Think, please, as you leave today: What happens if all we do about this subject is *get excited* about it, *talk* about it, and *don't* take action. What happens then?"

Tying the Closing to the Opening

- If it's a story you intentionally haven't quite finished in the body of your speech, *now* is the time to WOW the audience with the conclusion of that story.
- **Example:** "And that little girl I mentioned at the beginning of my talk; the one who didn't speak till she was two, and was judged to be "educably developmentally disabled" by more than one of her grade schoolteachers. Well, let me bring you up-to-date on what the special auditory software program helped her accomplish: Cassandra just delivered the valedictorian speech - at Yale!"

Use the Title of your speech in the Closing

- **Example**: If the title of your presentation was, "What's Holding *You* Back?" then an appropriate ending statement could easily be, "So, let me end my talk the way I began it, and ask the same question, 'What's Holding *You* Back?'

Stop – look at the audience – and enjoy the applause!

Now that we've discussed the **Content component** of *"No Sweat" Public Speaking!* (NSPS), it's time to talk about how that message is presented to the audience.

Delivery

The second component of the NSPS formula is **Delivery**.

Delivery is the presentation of the **Content** of your speech to the audience. It's presenting the information and the message you want them to consume.

As mentioned earlier, **Delivery** is more important - make that *far* more important - than the **Content** of your speech.

Your **Content** may be the best.

Your professional credentials - education, experience, papers published, etc. - may have you established as the preeminent expert in your field; however, if you can't *deliver* your message in an articulate and entertaining manner, your message will essentially go *undelivered*!

***Great delivery* is *essential* to a great speech.**

If you can't deliver a speech well, and many people can't, you might as well have your words printed and distribute them to the audience.

Better yet, *email* it to them. That will save you the embarrassment of facing the crowd!

The **Delivery component** of the speech has two parts: **Verbal** and **Nonverbal**.

FRED MILLER • *NO SWEAT* PUBLIC SPEAKING!

Verbal Delivery is your voice and how you use it.

Nonverbal Delivery, in this context, is about everything else you use in delivering your speech, excluding props, special effects, and others that we'll discuss later.

Before explaining the elements of these parts, let's review a previously made point that is germane to this discussion: ***Everything* must be in sync with your main message.**

I'm mentioning this again (remember repetition), because if the **Delivery** of your message is not in sync with the **Content**, you're presenting mixed messages. This is *not* a good thing. It thoroughly confuses and frustrates an audience and places you at risk of losing them.

There was a famous study done by UCLA professor, Albert Mehrabian, in the 1960's. He ran experiments with students to determine how we communicate. His findings were that we receive information in the following percentages:

- Nonverbal Communication - 55%
- Verbal Communication - 38%
- Words - 7%

For years, these percentages were held up to be the model for communicating to an audience. More recent research suggests that Dr. Mehrabian's audience was mostly students, and the findings are skewed to those participants. Students are only a small portion of people who receive and process information.

It's likely the differences are not as great as 55/38/7. While the percentages may be different, the fact remains that gestures, facial expressions, and other nonverbal body language conveys more than the way words are spoken. The way things are stated, i.e., verbal communication, carries more weight than the words that are spoken.

Important Facts
- Delivery trumps content.
- Nonverbal Delivery trumps Verbal Delivery.
- Content and Delivery *must* be in sync.

Nonverbal Communication

Words, and way they are conveyed, do not always deliver the exact message you want the recipient(s) to receive. Even if the verbal delivery is excellent, there can still be miscommunication.

If all you send is the audio message, there's a part missing that could be extremely important – the nonverbal part of your talk.

It's the difference between a phone call and a one-on-one, face-to-face meeting.

It's what you hear versus what you see and hear.

Would you rather listen to a speech on the radio or see and listen to it on television?

The meaning derived from just hearing versus seeing and hearing can be *significant*.

Take, for example, the famous 1960 Nixon-Kennedy Presidential debate. Those who heard the debate on the radio had Richard Nixon as the winner. Those who watched (and heard) it on television gave the most points to John Kennedy.

Nixon came across better on radio then did Kennedy. However, those looking at him on television saw a man with a five-o'clock shadow, ill-fitting shirt, and sweating forehead. He was pitted against a handsome, tanned, and a well-groomed younger man who won over the viewing audience, partially because of the image he projected.

This is one reason video teleconferencing has value over *just a phone call*. Be it a meeting, speaking event, or concert; *nothing* beats being there in person. That's the appeal, isn't it, of live concerts, live theater and live sporting events.

The Elements of **Nonverbal Communication** are:

- Eye contact
- Facial expressions
- Gestures
- Posture
- Body movement.

These expressions can be *voluntary*, but because they express emotion, they are often *involuntary*. This is one good reason you want to always read the expression on the faces in your audience. They may not be verbalizing their feelings to you, but they're certainly conveying them. It's incumbent upon *you*, the presenter, to pick up on these, analyze them, and adjust your talk as needed.

If there's ever confusion between your verbal and your non-verbal communications, the audience will choose the nonverbal as the dominant message. You've heard the expression, "Actions speak louder than words." They do!

Example: You might be talking about how excited you are about a product or service offering, and your voice and words indicate this. However, if you're leaning on the lectern, looking out the window while speaking, and are not expressive with your body language, the message the audience gets is the nonverbal communication you're presenting. Here, you're less than enthusiastic about your subject.

Even if you never open your mouth, nonverbal communication will deliver volumes of information to your audience. Ever see a professional mime perform? Wow!

All nonverbal communication, when performed in front of larger groups, should be *exaggerated* so the entire audience sees and better understands the points you are emphasizing. If you hold your hands up, hold them *way* up! If you stretch them out, stretch them *way* out!

All you Hams and Drama Queens– *now* is your time!

Let's take a look at each one of them closer.

EYE CONTACT

You've heard the expression, "It's all in the *eyes*." It *really is!*

Eye Contact is our first element of **Nonverbal Communication**.

After being introduced by the Master of Ceremonies, one of

the first things to do while taking a long pause *before* beginning your presentation, is to find several friendly faces in the audience.

A key reason for arriving early at the location where you will be presenting is to *Meet & Greet* audience members. Introduce yourself and ask them questions. You'll be able to better know *who* they are, *what* they know, *why* they are attending, and *what* they're expecting from *you*.

Another *Meet & Greet* benefit is that it will lessen your nervousness. It's much easier to talk to people you know, even if it's only been a brief *Meet & Greet*.

Initially, making eye contact with people you met beforehand who express friendliness and an eagerness to hear you speak, will get your talk off to a jump start.

It's a good idea to know *before* starting your talk who the first person you will be making eye contact with when you utter your first words.

Pause, look that person directly in the eye and start speaking. Then, after a few moments, move on to another welcoming face.

Eye Contact is one means of expressing that you have *confidence in your competence* and don't need to completely rely on notes for all the information you're distributing. Your knowledge is in your head. You know your stuff. Use those notes to refresh those facts for you.

By using good eye contact you can *connect with the audience*, a major goal of public speaking.

Eye Contact expresses honesty and sincerity. Language like, "Look me in the eye when you talk to me (or when I'm talking to you)," "Eyes are the window to the soul," and "I can read it in his eyes" confirm this belief.

They can also express fear, wonderment, openness, disgust, confusion and a variety of other human emotions. Look for these emotions in the faces of your audience and be keenly aware they will receive like messages from you when given.

Just like good conversations with individuals, eye contact makes them look at you and keeps their attention. Keep in mind that a great speech (you *do* want to give a *great* one, don't you?) *should be like a one-on-one conversation.* The difference is that only *you*, the presenter, are doing most of the talking.

This doesn't mean that you're not also *receiving* communication.

You are interacting with everyone, and it is a two-way street. Your eyes are one of the tools you use to catch and interpret the messages the crowd is giving you.

The expressions on the faces in the audience, the look and direction of their eyes, and their body posture and movement will indicate how well the communication is going.

Constantly make note of this as you look at the audience. It is vital feedback for you.

The responses you get may suggest changes you need to make in your delivery.

For instance, a number of faces indicating confusion about something you just presented suggest that you repeat, perhaps in a different manner, the point you want to make. Do this, and check again, the response the audience is giving to see whether you've cleared up the confusion.

(People yawning, snoring, drooling, or running for the exits are indications of *serious* problems with your speech!)

While it isn't possible to have individual eye contact with *everyone* in an audience, the following suggestions will work:

Use the *lighthouse effect* as you scan the crowd.

Modify it so you are as mechanical and predictable as those beacons are. Try looking at *quadrants* of the audience, and do it in a random fashion. Stop for a moment or two when you find a friendly face and make direct eye contact.

Don't linger on one person because you don't want to stare. If you're having eye contact with someone and they look away, move on to another face. You don't want to make someone feel uneasy. (Be aware that in some cultures, direct eye contact is not acceptable. In others, lowering the eyes actually signifies respect.)

By becoming skilled at using **Eye Contact** as you speak with a crowd, you are taking control of the presentation to make it do what you want it to do. Having control is a big key to success in public speaking.

One eye contact technique is to use the *one thought – one person* method. Make eye contact with someone until your thought is finished, then go on to another audience member with your next thought.

The people next to the person you're making eye contact with will also feel the connection.

Then, move on and find another friendly expression on someone's face and pause again for a few moments to make direct **Eye Contact**.

Continue **Eye Contact** communication throughout the speech.

Be aware, also, of the *involuntary* messages your eyes can deliver. This is especially true with small audiences, where they are close enough to easily see you, and large events where they might be projecting you onto a large screen.

- Blinking too frequently suggests discomfort and may indicate dishonesty.
- Rolling your eyes, especially after a question is asked, can convey that you thought the question was silly or inappropriate. (You *don't* want to do this!)

Tips:
Let's not forget these eye expressions:
- Staring
- Crying
- Winking
- Squinting
- Twitching
- Closing the eyes
- *Squeezing* the eyes shut
- Making your eyes look down, up and sideways

Practice looking in a mirror, raising your eyebrows, squinting, opening your eyes wide, and even rolling your eyes. (If you have children, you'll have seen this expression and *know* what it means!) These expressions will have to be exaggerated when in front of a large audience.

Before you speak, look into full-length mirror. Besides checking out your hair, suit, teeth, etc., look carefully at your face, including your eyes. If your eyes are red because of allergies, smoke, or for other reasons, consider using eye drops to take away the redness.

While everyone can't see the whites of your eyes, it will make a difference to those who can. The added relief the drops provide will keep the irritation from being an added distraction to you.

We now go beyond the eyes to the whole face for the next element of **Nonverbal** communication: **Facial expressions**.

FACIAL EXPRESSIONS

We've heard people say things like; "I can read his face," or, "The look on her face told the whole story."

Those impressions are correct! Our faces express emotion in various ways, but the interpretations are mostly universal.

The first and most important **Facial expression** is – a **smile!**

A **Smile** definitely *is* universal.

It makes people feel liked and gives the impression you care about them.

A **Smile** can *instantly* put people, including your audience, at ease.

It conveys warmth.

It's a powerful expression that communicates friendliness no matter what language people speak or where they come from. We look for babies to smile at us, don't we?

It can also, almost instantly, make *you* feel better and ease any tension you might have. (Keep this in mind when the butterflies in your stomach start flying.)

I refer to a smile as a *nonphysical* hug.

Here's the analogy: One of the neat things about a hug is when you give one – you get one right back! The same results often come with smiling!

It was this connection that lead me to pick the Smile Train (www.smiletrain.org/) to receive a portion of the profits of the sale of this book. Smile Train is a nonprofit organization that is focused on solving a single problem: cleft lip and palate. In developing countries there are millions of children who are suffering with unrepaired clefts. Most cannot eat or speak properly. They aren't allowed to attend school or hold a job. Furthermore, they face very difficult lives filled with shame and isolation, pain, and heartache. The great work of Smile Train is being done in 78 of the world's poorest countries.

Smiling translates into happiness, and it's contagious!

Of course, other expressions can be made with your face. These can involve more than just your mouth and eyes.

Take a few moments, please, and picture the following expressions in your mind's eye. Better yet, stand in front of a mirror and make your face express these emotions:

- Disgust
- Happy
- Sad
- Embarrassed
- Surprised
- Nervous
- Devious
- Tastes Great
- Tired
- Sleepy
- Sour
- Goofy

- Thoughtful
- Confused
- Angry
- Frustration
- Anticipation
- Sick
- Confident

Interesting, isn't it, how much we can communicate without saying a word?

Other facial expressions, often involuntary, but important to be aware of include:

- Yawning – sleepy, bored
- Pursing lips – to hold back emotion
- Tearing up and crying - emotion
- Sweating – feeling uneasy
- Blushing – embarrassed, ill at ease
- Raising eyebrows – surprised, shocked

And . . . "with a wink and a nod" we can easily convey a message to those we're communicating with.

Besides the facial expressions we can make, there are other aspects of our face we should be aware of, and the messages they might be sending.

The general appearance of our face is something we don't have much control over, but we should make the most of what we have!

Hair

- The first and easiest thing to do, is to be certain that our hair is clean, neat and groomed. Women are far better, and have more flexibility with this than men, but we all need to look in the mirror, and present our best appearance.
- Men, if they have a mustache or beard, should have it trimmed.

Makeup

- Women should wear a bit of makeup, being certain to skip anything that's glittery or shiny. Bright light will emphasize this.
- Men might also consider using a blemish stick or bit of makeup. (Remember: Nixon lost the Presidential Debate to Kennedy partially because of the nonverbal message his five o'clock shadow was sending.)
- Most people, when appearing on television, will have makeup applied. This is more important now because of HD television. I remember a producer of our local public television station commenting on the switch from analog to digital, "For you, the viewer, the transition is seamless. For me, it's *better makeup!*" Sometimes, for large audiences, the speaker is projected onto giant monitors, so the same rules of makeup might apply.

Teeth

- Check them for food left from the meal before speaking, and women should check them for any lipstick that might be there. (A small pocketknife with a built-in toothpick can be handy!)

Earring and necklaces

- They shouldn't speak louder than the speaker wearing them. Conservatism is the goal here. If jewelry is shiny, light might bounce off it and be a distraction.

Other things to note

- It's a good idea to study a video of you making a presentation. Some people have involuntary twitches that might be brought on by the anxiety of a speech. Others possess habits, nervous and otherwise, that can be seen on tape and corrected when presenting.
- **Example:** Winking at audience members, unless used for a special effect, should be avoided. (Did I hear someone say, "Sarah Palin?")

All speakers are served well by having their appearance, before the presentation, checked out by someone they trust. A full length mirror and good lighting is valuable here. Also, always have a small hand mirror with you for those last minute checks.

GESTURES

If I place my index finger, vertically in front of my closed lips, you know what I'm asking the audience to do, correct? ("Please be quiet.")

Have you ever seen the picture of three monkeys: one with his eyes covered, one with his ears covered and one with his mouth covered? The meaning these three gestures convey is: "See no evil, Hear no evil, and Speak no evil."

Gestures, like other forms of nonverbal communication, can stand on their own when communicating a message. They can also be combined with other forms of nonverbal communication, or be used in conjunction with the verbal part of speech delivery.

Gestures are not confined to the hands and movements we make with them. **Gestures** are defined as motion of the limbs or body made to express or help express thought or to emphasize speech.

Think about signing for babies and hearing impaired, coaching signals in sports, and the communications runway people give pilots on the tarmac. These are all examples of using gestures, voluntarily, for very specific communication objectives.

Gestures allow us to express a variety of thoughts and feelings.

Examples:

- Throwing hands in the air – "I give up!"
- Moving a hand forcefully up and down – Making a point.
- Zipping one's lips shut – "Quiet"
- Snapping fingers – "I just remembered!"
- Head in hands – Worry.
- Tapping on chest or head - "In my heart," and "On my mind".
- Shrugging the shoulders – "I don't know," or "Who cares?"
- Cocking the head in a specific direction – "It's over there," or "Let's go."
- Pounding a fist into the palm of your hand – "I'm mad!"
- Holding your stomach – "I'm not feeling well."
- Rubbing the stomach – "Tastes good!"

Important: Gestures are *not* universal!

Different cultures interpret gestures in different manners. A seemingly innocuous gesture in this country could well be an obscene, and even insulting gesture, in another culture.

With our country growing increasingly culturally diverse, it's important to be aware of this. Being insensitive to this could negate an otherwise good presentation. Do your research and check out the different meanings of gestures *before* using them.

Example: *Thumbs Up* is a common gesture in the US. It is done with a closed fist, and the thumb extended upward. Doing this indicates *great!*, *awesome!*, or indicates approval. In a number of cultures, this gesture carries a similar meaning. However, the gesture is considered rude and even obscene in Iran and Iraq and has no meaning in Turkey.

Exercise: Go back to the expression list you just pictured in your mind, or mimicked in the mirror, and add **Gestures to indicate the following feelings**. (Really, do it now – I'll be here when you get back!)

- Disgust
- Happy
- Sad
- Embarrassed
- Surprised
- Nervous
- Devious
- Tastes Great
- Tired
- Sleepy
- Sour

- Goofy
- Thoughtful
- Confused
- Angry
- Frustration
- Anticipation
- Sick
- Confident

(I hope you *really* stopped to do it and didn't just continue reading!) Even more interesting than the first exercise, wasn't it?

Additional Tips about **Gestures**:

Don't point.
Pointing with the index finger is considered rude. It reminds people of their childhood and being scolded by their parents. It implies that the speaker is trying to convince the audience of something that may not be true. (Bill Clinton, "I did not...")

Be aware that:
- Open hands indicate openness, and crossed arms show the opposite.
- A clenched fist can indicate anger and frustration.

An important rule I want to reiterate here is that gestures and other expressions *must be in sync* with the total message and feel comfortable. Just as delivery trumps content, nonverbal trumps verbal. Gestures should appear natural and comfortable. Sometimes *ap-*

pearing comfortable means *practicing* being comfortable. Some-times, it means *many* practice sessions.

Just like a professional athlete, carpenter, painter, or musician makes their performances appear easy, you, as a speaker, must practice – practice – practice. (More on practicing later.)

The larger the room you're speaking in, the more exaggerated your gestures should be. Similarly, if you're speaking with a small group, your gestures should be smaller.

When not gesturing, let your arms hang loosely next to your body. This signals you are at ease with your message and its pre-sentation.

Suggestion: Watch television or a movie with the sound turned *off!* It will give you some great insight into *all* the non-verbal communication elements that should be used in your speech.

POSTURE

Posture is the next **Nonverbal** element.

There's one chance to make a first impression.

You'll make that impression on the audience as the Master of Cer-emonies ends your introduction and you start walking to the lectern.

Walk with *deliberate steps* that give the nonverbal message to your audience that *you* are about to take over the meeting, and will be in charge during your turn at the lectern.

Do this with your shoulders straight and your head held high.

Be aware, you *may* make that first impression earlier if you're seated, before being introduced, when you're visible to the audience.

Important: If you're a scheduled speaker, *consider yourself on stage even when you're not!*

Especially if people can see you, be certain to sit with good posture: back straight, feet planted on the floor, and arms relaxed on your lap. Do not slouch

Be attentive, and look at the other speakers during their presentations. Don't fidget or read your material while others are taking their turn at the lectern.

It's important, for several reasons, to listen to speakers who precede you.

- First, you may be able to tag onto something another speaker says. This could be effective in driving home a particular point.
- Second, they may talk about something similar to what you plan to present. If so, you might want to make minor adjustments in your talk to differentiate your message.
  - » This is one of the best reasons, where making points in the body of your speech, to use *personal* stories. *No one* but *you* can tell *your* story! Unless, of course, you give them permission to. (Be certain they give you credit for it!)
- Finally, it's the polite thing to do. You might learn something!

When you arrive at the spot where you'll begin your talk, pause for a long moment, look out and briefly survey the audience. Find the friendly face of someone you met when you arrived early to *Meet and Greet - then* speak your opening words.

Your feet should point straight ahead, about shoulder length apart.

Your Posture is important and coveys a message.

- *Good, straight* **Posture** indicates leadership and confidence.
  - » It tells the audience that *you* are in control. It conveys the message that you have *confidence in your competence.*
- *Leaning slightly forward* shows the audience you care.
- *Slouching to one side* delivers the opposite message. It shows disinterest.
- *Hunched shoulders* indicate lack of confidence and possibly low self-esteem.
- *For an emotional speech,* try puffing yourself up.
  - » We do that when we're feeling aggressive and ready to fight. (You've probably seen different animals do this, haven't you?)
- *If you want to feel relaxed,* assume a **Posture** that reflects that feeling. (This, combined with some deep breathing *will* relax you!)

Some *Dos* and *Don'ts* about Posture:

Don't jingle!

- Putting one or both hands into your pockets and jingling loose change or keys is a nervous habit some people fall into.
- It's distracting to the audience and takes away from your message.

- A good tip is to leave change, keys and everything else you normally carry in your pockets, somewhere safe when you're speaking.

Don't fidget.
- Even if your hands are not in your pockets, don't rub nails or fingers together or engage in any other type of fidgeting.

No Fig Leaf stance.
- Hands crossed in front of you at the crotch, or over your rear end, or anywhere else, indicates non-openness.
- The military *At Ease* position, crossing your arms in front of you or clasping hands in front or behind you should also be avoided.

Don't rock from your heels to your toes.
- This will distract the audience and interfere with your message.

Don't sway!
- I remember one of my Toastmasters Meetings where the speaker was a college professor. Delivering his speech from behind the lectern, he swayed from side to side. I was his Evaluator that evening, and I started off mimicking his swaying and asked, "Michael, did you ever spend any time *on a ship?*"
  - » **Important:** I would *not* have made this remark had I not known Michael well. He was an accomplished and experienced speaker who just got into a silly groove. Like most Toastmasters, Michael attended meetings and regularly

spoke to *improve* his talks. He *sought* productive comments.

» A good speaker evaluation will tell the speaker what they did well and give suggestions for areas that can be improved.

» Merely stroking speakers with kudos may build their egos, but it won't help them improve their Content or Delivery - the reasons they joined Toastmasters.

» Many members consider the Evaluation Part of the meeting to be the most important and productive part.

Don't lean on the lectern.

• It conveys a too-relaxed attitude and gives the impression that you don't care.

Don't cross your arms.

• People do that when they are feeling defensive. Be especially aware of this during your Q&A session. If you do this, the audience will pick up on it, and it is not the message you want them to receive.

Do hold your head high and your chin slightly up.

• This gives the audience the impression that you're in control. (Watch clips of President Obama for good examples of this.)

Don't look down.

• I know, I know - that's where your notes are!

• Try to briefly glance to check your note, then look at the audience. This is another reason to use a Mind Map, with pictures and symbols, rather than linear notes to deliver your talk.

Good posture should be natural and relaxed, not stiff and tense. Perfecting this element, like other elements of your delivery, verbal and nonverbal, takes practice.

Practice in front of a mirror, ask friends to evaluate this nonverbal part of your talk, and look at your posture on videos of your talks.

Picture this: The Master of Ceremonies just finished introducing you.

Now, it's *Your* turn! Rise from your seat, stand tall and walk deliberately to stage center.

Stop.

Pause.

WOW them!

BODY MOVEMENT

The last **Nonverbal** skill is **Body Movement**.

Picture this: The six foot, five inch, python-armed bar bouncer just spotted someone in the club he ejected the previous night. The baby-faced kid had shown a counterfeit ID while trying to purchase a beer. Now that punk is holding a Bud Light up to his mouth.

How do you picture the bouncer's body movement as he clears a way for himself through the crowded bar and heads toward the underage drinker?

If the kid sees the bouncer before he reaches him, do you think he'll *get the message?* You bet!

That kind of Body Movement definitely conveys a message, and no spoken communication is needed, is it?

Body movement, alone, or combined with other elements of nonverbal communication, can send messages to your audience with no words uttered.

As with *all* your **Delivery, Body Movement** *must be in sync* with the total message. If there's a discrepancy, **Body Movement** will take precedence. (Kind of like the person who gets stopped by the police, says he has no contraband in the vehicle, but is sweating bullets, twitching, and generally nervous. Does the police officer believe his words or the message his body is sending?)

Important points about Body Movement:

- The larger the audience, the more exaggerated your body movements should be.
- Know where you are, and where you want to be.
- Don't wander off to one side of the stage and stay there.
- Usually, come back to where you started speaking, usually stage center or behind a lectern placed at one side of the stage.
- The lectern, placed at one side of the stage, is often used when delivering a PowerPoint presentation.
- Most presentations are conducted at center stage. (Sometimes, there's an X on the stage that marks the spot you should continually return to.)
- Just as you shouldn't sway behind a lectern, don't pace back and forth across the stage

- Your audience's attention will be focused on the pacing and not on the message.
- You don't want them to feel like they're watching a ping pong match!
- When you move, unless it's for emphasis, move *slowly*.
- If possible, and it usually is, don't turn your back on the audience.
- If you must turn your back, perhaps after walking into the audience as part of your presentation, don't start speaking until you turn around. Even if you have a microphone, when you turn your back you risk losing your, and the audience's nonverbal communication. It's not worth the risk. Let those silent moments, until you can face the people, be a chance for them to absorb what they have seen and heard.
- Don't walk backwards to prevent turning your back. You might trip – that would be worse.

What body movement images do the following place in the "movie in your mind"?
- Someone just matched all six numbers of the Lottery.
- Someone just matched all but the last number of the Lottery.
- A golfer sinks a long, long, *l-o-o-o-n-g* putt and wins the tournament.
- The boxing match was close. The referee is holding one arm of each fighter as the announcer declares, "And the winner is . . ."
- Someone is playing the *air guitar* to the Moody Blues' song, Your Wildest Dreams!

Bottom Line: Your **Body Movement** can communicate!

OTHER ELEMENTS OF NONVERBAL COMMUNICATION

The clothing and accessories you wear are also elements of non-verbal communication.

As a rule, the clothes you choose should take into account your audience, the event you're speaking at, and your message.

Wearing a uniform, such as a doctor's white jacket or a nurse's uniform, immediately conveys a message to the audience.

A speaker who comes out wearing a pith helmet or cowboy hat will also make an impression.

Also, a military or law enforcement uniform, and the insignias that indicate the individual's rank, provide associations the audience can immediately connect with and make pre-speech assumptions.

Generally, speakers should dress above their audience. This will set you a bit apart from the audience. It will elevate you in their eyes and boost your self-confidence.

Under-dressing or a slovenly appearance will have the opposite effect. It might even convey a certain amount of arrogance on your part. There are exceptions. Steve Jobs always wears blue jeans, sneakers, and a black turtleneck. This is really part of his *personal brand*, and no one questions his appearance. He also has something that let's him break the *dress code* rule. *I* don't have, and you may not either - and that's *charisma!*

Conservative suits for both sexes, are best. Think about what newscasters wear for their evening broadcasts. They always look crisp, clean, and are conservatively dressed. They have news to deliver and don't want their appearance to be the news.

The same goes for accessories like jewelry, ties, scarves, and watches. Flashy, figuratively and literally, in those areas ends as being a distraction to your message.

Conservative and well groomed also applies to personal grooming: hair, nails, makeup, etc.

Shoes should be shined.

Loose threads should be cut, and dangling buttons sewed.

All clothing should be checked for spots, dirt and lint. (Remember – HD TV!)

You look professional. Part of looking professional is that your appearance doesn't distract from your message.

Everything should be in sync to help the audience **GET IT!**

Finally, *before speaking,* do a quick full mirror check, front and back, to catch a potential embarrassment before speaking.

Verbal Communication

The other part of delivery is - **Verbal Communication**.

Verbal Communication is your voice and how you use it.

The elements of **Verbal Communication** are:
- Pronunciation and Enunciation
- Projection
- Inflection
- Cadence
- Pause

PRONUNCIATION AND ENUNCIATION

The first element of verbal communication is **Pronunciation and Enunciation: Pronounce** all words correctly and **enunciate** clearly and distinctly!

If you don't do this, you might as well be a mime! Plus, you had best become *a very good one!*

Sounds simple, doesn't it? Unfortunately, it's one of the verbal elements speakers sometimes don't do well, and many aren't even aware of it.

No matter how great your **Content** is, if you stand in front of people and mumble and mispronounce words, your message will very quickly be lost and it will be impossible to regain attention.

If you're not sure how a word is pronounced, or if you're using it in the correct context, look it up online. Some online dictionaries have an audio file that will pronounce it for you. It's also advisable to check several sources.

People with strong regional dialects and those who speak English as their second language need to be especially aware of this potential roadblock to good communication.

I know a doctor from another country whom, during his residency, was asked by a patient for a different doctor *because he couldn't understand what the physician was saying.*

The doctor took the patient's comment to heart. He joined Toastmasters and threw himself into their program. It worked! I was with him several years later, and he spoke extremely well!

Some of this **Pronunciation and Enunciation** element goes hand-in-glove with the **Speaking Tip** to always *avoid: Buzz Words,* also known as *jargon.* Buzz words and jargon, according to the dictionary, are words or phrases connected with a specialized field or group that usually sounds important or technical and are used primarily to impress laypeople. It's not just businesses that have them. Buzz words can also be found within specific cultural and generational groups and organizations.

If people hear a word or phrase that they're not familiar with or if they can't understand what you are saying at all, their brains shift into *Sherlock Holmes mode* and they struggle to figure out what you're trying to say.

Whether they figure it out or not, they will miss your next remarks trying to make sense of those statements. Sometimes they give up and tune you out altogether. If that happens they look forward to your closing - so they can leave!

Again, our goal is that we want the audience to **GET IT!** If they can't understand the words, acronyms, and phrases they hear, they'll quickly turn off the presenter.

PROJECTION

The second element of **Verbal Communication** is **Projection**.

Even when your **Pronunciation and Enunciation** are flawless, it won't make a bit of difference if your audience can't hear you.

Generally, people don't speak loud enough. If you combine low volume with a fast delivery, often because of nervousness, and/or excitement, the odds of your audience **Getting It!** drop dramatically.

Nobody enjoys straining to hear a presenter.

At the other end of the projection spectrum, people don't like being yelled at, either.

Projecting your voice *loudly* and *clearly* is important to gaining attention and respect. Actors are instructed to "talk to the folks in the last row." This way, people sitting up front don't get all the attention and those behind them don't get neglected.

To help accomplish this, look at the back wall and mentally note that your voice must carry all the way to that location.

This doesn't mean you should yell! Simply speak as though you were talking to someone sitting (or standing) several feet away.

Here's a practice exercise for voice projection. You'll need a partner:

- Practice speaking with your partner as you sit or stand a comfortable distance apart, as though you were having a normal conversation.
- Then, you and your partner each back up three or four steps. Continue talking.
- Keep taking a few steps back until you and your partner are backed up against opposite walls. Continue talking.
- Keep practicing until you feel comfortable speaking (not shouting) and your partner can hear you clearly.

Consistent practice like this (and even singing in the shower) will improve your **Projection.** Just like exercising other muscles, your vocal cords ability to project will get stronger with use.

Also, as with other muscles, your vocal cords can be strained and damaged. The same rules that apply to any athletic endeavor apply here, also. Start slowly, don't overdo it, and if injured, seek medical attention.

Proper breathing is essential to voice **Projection** and to staying calm. Make sure you are breathing from the diaphragm. It's also a good idea to do some breathing exercises before starting your speech so that your voice is relaxed and tension-free. When you exhale, you relieve stress. That's what happens when we sigh.

Sometimes enlisting the help of a professional voice coach is a good idea. Their advice and coaching can make a significant difference in your projection and hence, your delivery.

Some people are blessed with great voices that can be heard by the last person in an auditorium with no audio system needed. I recall a member of my Toastmaster club who was in the seminary. He had a *great* baritone voice. It was easy to see him on the altar someday delivering a sermon. Most of us don't have that gift.

If needed and available, use a sound system. It is not always a matter of plug-and-play. If unfamiliar with the technology of the system you'll be using, get some tech help for adjusting it to work best for you.

Make sure to practice with it first. Your voice will sound different when projected electronically, and it takes a bit of getting used to.

The three main types of microphones used are:
- Attached to the lectern
- Hand-held
- Lavaliere

Each has advantages and disadvantages.

If the microphone is attached to the lectern, unless you remove it from its holder, you'll be tempted to stand behind it. This minimizes your ability to speak using important **Nonverbal** communication skills **Body Movements** and **Gestures.**

There's also the temptation for some to lean on the lectern and even cross their feet. This relaxed stance can send a nonprofessional message to the audience.

Hand-held microphones can be corded or cordless.

They can also be used effectively or ineffectively. If not used correctly, they'll detract from a good presentation. Have you ever seen someone gesture with both hands, microphone in one, while they continue talking? You can see - I should say, hear, or don't hear - what I mean, right?

When the mike is corded, guard against tripping over the cord, fidgeting with it, wrapping it around the lectern, etc.

The answer might be to use a lavaliere microphone. One hint here – *don't* thump your chest! (I've done it – *not* cool!)

Also, remove, or turn *off* your lavaliere microphone before having private conversations, going to the restroom, or doing anything else that might later prove embarrassing!

If you're naturally soft-spoken, it might be good to invest in a small portable system. There are a number of fine, lightweight ones available.

With *any* sound system, it's important to **practice** with the equipment prior to speaking, if possible. Best, also, to *demand* a mike check! You have to get used to using the equipment and listening to yourself *before* presenting before an audience. It's best to test and practice a sound system in the room where you'll be speaking. Each room has its own issues, and sound projection can be one of them.

We've all been in spaces where you can't clearly hear the person sitting across from you. It is to be hoped the place you'll be speaking in won't be this bad, but finding out things like this in advance, and managing it well, can save the day for your talk.

It's also a good idea to have the Master of Ceremonies check the audience to ask if they can hear clearly. If not, perhaps some will want to move to a different seat before the program gets going.

INFLECTION

The third **element** of **Verbal Delivery** is **Inflection** or **Voice Modulation.**

Did you ever hear a speaker who spoke in a monotone? (Did I hear someone say, "R2D2" of *Star Wars* fame?) If you did, you probably couldn't wait for his or her talk to end, and it's doubtful you remember anything about it.

Inflection is one element that keeps the audience alert, engaged, and eager for more. It is a *change in the pitch or tone of the voice.* Varying your tone throughout the speech - raising your voice slightly to indicate a question, lowering it to end a declarative sentence, speaking louder to indicate excitement or softer to express sadness.

There are several kinds of **Inflection**. Let's look at each of them:

Upward Inflection
- This is when there is a change in pitch going from a *lower to a higher note* within the vowel.
- Most often, this change in pitch indicates questioning, insincerity, surprise, or suspense.
- **Examples:** Raise the pitch at the end of these words, keeping in mind what they convey with a downward (opposite) inflection:

>> No!

>> Wow!

>> Really?

>> Amazing!

Downward Inflection

- This is when there is a change in pitch going from a *higher to a lower note* within the vowel.
- Most often, this change in pitch indicates confidence, finality, power, and certainty.
- **Examples:** Lower the pitch at the end of these words, keeping in mind what they convey with an upward (opposite) inflection:

  >> Done

  >> No

  >> Go

  >> Got it

Level Inflection

- This is when there is *no change in pitch* within the vowel.
- Most often, this indicates disinterest and indecision.
- **Examples:** Don't vary the pitch in these words:

  >> OK

  >> Maybe

  >> Fine

  >> Whatever

  >> Sure

Double or Circumflex Inflection

- This is when there is a *rising and falling,* or a *falling and rising of pitch* within the vowel.
- Most often, this change in pitch indicates confidence, finality, power, and certainty.
- **Examples:** Lower the pitch at the end of these words, keeping in mind what they convey with a downward inflection:
  - » Done!
  - » No!
  - » Go!
  - » Amazing!
  - » We're finished here!

Lowering your inflection at the end of a sentence makes it more powerful and gives the audience the impression you believe your own message.

Use *upward* inflections in the middle of a sentence to make the sentence more interesting and bring some attention to your point.

It's important to vary the pitch. It will help keep your audience in tune (no pun intended!) with your message and help them understand its substance.

Try the following exercise to demonstrate the importance of this in your delivery. Say slowly, and out loud, this sentence: "I did not say he lost the keys."

Each time you say it, put the **Inflection** on the underlined word.

Exercise:
- "I did not say he lost the keys."
  (If not you, who said it?)
- "I did not say he lost the keys."
  (Maybe you wrote it?)
- "I did not say he lost the keys."
  (I guess someone else lost the keys.)
- "I did not say he lost the keys."
  (Perhaps he gave them away?)
- "I did not say he lost the keys."
  (Gee! I hope he didn't lose the car!)

Amazing, isn't it, how the entire meaning of a sentence can change by inflecting one of its words? Use this tool in delivering your speech and you'll see fewer yawning faces in the audience!

One excellent way to get the attention of the audience is to *lower* your voice. It's a pattern interrupt that sends out the message, "Listen – *This* is important!"

This technique is particularly effective if you're speaking with excitement and passion, and suddenly pause . . . lower your voice, and speak, " . . ."

The quieter your voice gets; the more important the message is perceived to be.

The idea is analogous to telling secrets. We lower our voice, and the recipient *must* listen more intently.

This has to be done naturally and sparingly, or the effect will be minimal. Done correctly and you can create a WOW! moment for your audience!

For a great description and some helpful exercises, hints and tips from a professional voice coach, read Dr. Candice Coleman's white paper on Using Inflection: www.sayitwell.com/Using_Inflections.html

CADENCE

Cadence, a natural partner of inflection, is our next element. It's the rhythmic flow of the words used when speaking.

Other terms used for this element are: meter, beat, measure, pace, and pulse.

Usually, and largely because of nervousness, presenters speak too quickly. I've written fifteen-minute speeches that I completed in half the time!

Some speakers think their enthusiasm, and passion for their subject is expressed by speaking quickly, and to a certain extent this is true.

Unfortunately, the result of a continued and too rapid speech pattern is that the audience is not given enough time for the information to sink in, and they often don't **GET IT!**

If the speaking pace is too rapid, the recipients have to work excessively hard to keep up. They won't do this for long because it's not fun to work that hard to understand a speaker. After a while, they'll just stop listening, and never **GET IT!**

At the other end of the spectrum, you don't want to speak *too slowly*. A very slow-paced delivery risks losing your audience's attention, also.

You also don't want to speak in a *staccato, rapid-fire* manner. This can equally off-putting.

Picture a military officer barking orders at his troops like: *"At-tention! - At-Ease! - Present Arms!"*

Varying the speed of your delivery along with appropriate **Inflection** and **Pauses** will keep the audience's attention up, and their eyes open.

Find a computer that has text-to-speech capabilities and experiment with different voices at different speeds. What you'll hear is a good reminder of the importance of your voice in delivering your message.

Another good exercise is to listen to, and read along with, great speeches. The audio and text can usually be found on line. Pick speakers you admire, and you'll better your **Cadence** and other speaking qualities.

Listen, also, to just the audio of talks you've given. Evaluate your own **Cadence**, and make any necessary adjustments in future speeches.

PAUSE

The last element of good verbal communication is the **Pause**.

It's the *last* element of our verbal communication skills discussion, but it should be the *first* thing you do when reaching the lectern, or center stage, after the Master of Ceremonies introduces you.

Standing in silence before the audience and looking out and scanning the crowd conveys an aura of authority and confidence. **Pause**, *almost* so long they might start thinking something is wrong. (It's a great time for a last moment of positive self-talk like, "I'm going to make this audience *rock!*")

Finally, when you *know* they're beginning to wonder - open your speech. *This* can be an extremely effective technique for capturing the audience's attention immediately.

Many speakers, especially those who are inexperienced, make the mistake of memorizing their speeches word-for-word and then reciting them as quickly as they can, without stopping even to take a breath. An experienced speaker knows to **Pause** periodically to give the audience time to catch up, and to let the meaning of what he or she is saying sink in. They need time to search their memory banks to see where the content you just presented fits for them. Sometimes what you deliver does not register at all. Be assured that if the statement is profound enough, some in the audience will even repeat it to themselves in their own words.

Pauses can be powerful. They are very important.

Claude Debussy, the famous French composer, said, "Music is the silence between the notes."

That analogy can be applied to speaking. Without a break, the delivery would be one long, continuous discourse without adequate time for the audience to take in and think about the message. When giving a humorous speech, you want to give the audience time to laugh at your joke without missing the next one!

Pauses separate thoughts. A good rule of thumb is to pause periodically to allow folks to absorb the message you have delivered up to that point.

A **Pause** builds anticipation. It gets the audience wondering, "What's coming next?"

Pausing, after asking the audience a question, makes them think and mentally involves them in your speech.

Never let your **Pause** be so long the audience thinks you have lost your place or are unsure what to say next.

Pausing, for most speakers, is tough to do. We tend to want to fill dead air with noise. Often, a speaker will fill the silence with filler words like, "Ah," "You know," "OK," "Like," and others.

If you find yourself using these fillers, it's a perfect time to catch yourself and say - *nothing!*

When searching for a word while speaking, rather than utter, "Umm" or "Ah" - **Pause.** Don't look down or up while **Pausing,** but look at an individual and start talking, again, when the word or phrase comes to mind. In Toastmasters, there is a person assigned to be an "Ah" counter. Their job is to ring a bell, or click a clicker whenever a speaker uses "Ah," "Umm," or other fillers. This makes the individual aware of this habit so their speaking improves. (Of course, the bell, or clicks stop after a specified number of rings.)

Practice **Pausing,** then breathing at the end of phrases where you've made a significant point. You'll feel better, and your audience will benefit, also.

Also, consider using the **Spontaneous Pause.** (It *will* seem spontaneous to the audience because you've rehearsed it so well!) If you stop yourself part way into a statement, pause, then go in another direction, that next set of statements can be powerful.

Example: In the closing of one of my talks, I say, "The next time someone gives you the opportunity to speak, (Pause) Check that statement! *Don't* wait for the opportunity – *Seek it out!* Look for it at your . . ."

You *do* want them to *get* your message – correct? So ......
Pause!

That's the *No Sweat* Public Speaking! Formula!

Let's quickly review and put the formula in outline form before moving on:

A Speech has **Two Components:**

1. Content
- **Title**
- **Introduction**
  - » Why this subject?
  - » Why this speaker?
  - » Why now?
- **Opening**
  - » Grab the audience's attention
  - » Tell them what you're going to tell them
- **Body**
  - » Tell Them
  - » Three to five main points with stories, preferably personal ones, to support those points

- **Conclusion**
  - » Tell them what you told them.
  - » Strong Closing.

2. **Delivery**
- **Nonverbal Communication**
  - » Eye Contact
  - » Facial Expressions
  - » Gestures
  - » Posture
  - » Body Movement
- **Verbal Communication**
  - » Pronunciation and Enunciation
  - » Projection
  - » Inflection
  - » Cadence
  - » Pause

Practice Your Speech

One of the questions I'm often asked is this: "If you had to give one piece of advice to someone who wants to improve their presentation skills, what would it be?"

My answer, after asking the audience to take out a piece of paper and have a pen is: "Speak!" "Speak!" "Speak!" "Speak!"

If you want to be a runner - *Run.*
If you want to be a chef - *Cook.*
If you want to be a speaker - *Speak!*

We've all heard, "**Practice** makes perfect."

No, it doesn't!

Perfect **Practice** makes perfect. However, don't ever expect your speech and its delivery to ever be perfect!

I once read a quote, "The road to perfection never ends."

I don't know who said it, but I completely agree.

Sports coaches tell their teams they'll "play as they **Practice**." Yes, **Practice** *is* that important!

You learn by doing - Period!

You can do all the intellectualizing you want. You can think about it, visualize, and think about it some more. But the *only* way to become a good speaker, or anything else you've set as a goal is, to **do it!**

Good educators know the **learning is in the doing.**

David Sandler wrote one great sales book, "You Can't Teach a Kid to Ride a Bicycle in a Seminar." That wisdom can be applied to speaking, also.

To become a good presenter, you must present! It's also mandatory, if you want to improve, to get critiques of your presentations. The content and delivery must be evaluated. A good coaching evaluation includes critiquing of each specific element of the speech and offers suggestions for improvement.

Hiring a professional coach makes sense for many who want to improve their presentation skills. The fact is this: **Professionals *have* coaches - Amateurs *don't*.**

Malcom Gladwell, in his book, *Outliers*, talks about things that make a person successful.

He says, "**Practice** isn't the thing you do *once* you're good. It's the thing you do that *makes* you good."

The same rule applies to your public speaking.

Gladwell says it takes **ten thousand hours of practice to become an expert.**

The first person I thought about when I read that was Michael Phelps, the Olympic swimming champion, who won 14 Olympic gold medals. He truly can be considered the best of the best.

His successes didn't come without an extraordinary amount of effort, dedication, and personal sacrifice. Ten thousand hours is an amazing amount of time, and I've got to assume that Michael

Phelps put in a minimum of that. When his friends were hanging out, socializing and having fun - Phelps was in the pool. When others his age were traveling, watching movies, or just relaxing with friends and family – he was in the pool. When other people his age were . . . – well, you've got the idea.

The Michael Phelps' example came to mind as we were experiencing the 2010 winter Olympics in Vancouver, Canada. None of the athletes in those games got to compete at that level on a whim and a prayer. They had worked and worked and worked some more at getting better in their chosen sport. They are the best of the best in their field. Many have left friends, family and even their homeland to work with single-minded determination on their goal. Not all will receive medals for all their sacrifices, but they will all be better for the effort that is made.

S-o-o-o-o-o – **Practice – practice – practice!**

Let's discuss several ways to practice.

Use a **Mind Map**
- This is one of the *best* ways to practice and improve your speech.
  - » Review your Mind Map carefully.
  - » Look at each graphic, symbol, and key word.
  - » Reinforce, in your mind, *why* you chose it and what point or story it's a reminder of. (If you can't quickly recall what the symbol or key word stood for, change it to something that is easily remembered and triggers instant recall.
  - » Look away from the Mind Map and try to re-create the map in your mind's eye.

» Repeat this process until you can *see* the Speech Mind Map without viewing it.

- One of the great benefits of using a Mind Map to deliver your talk is that the entire speech can be on one sheet of paper. Merely glance at the map and you'll easily know where you are in your talk.
  » You'll also easily be able to recall the point for reinforcing.
  » Many find this is better than looking at black and white text.
  » It is also easier if, for a variety of reasons, you have to modify your speech at the last minute or on-the-fly. Your talk is already in modules, so adjustments can be made quickly.

Use an **Audio Recorder**

- You may not recognize your voice the first time! I know I hardly did, and quickly realized where I need to improve,
- Listen at home or when you are driving and have windshield time.
- Pay close attention to the verbal elements of your speech.
  » **Pronunciation and Enunciation** – are you easily understood? Are your words delivered clearly and distinctly or would people verbally or mentally be saying, "Huh?"
    › How does your voice sound?
    › As previously mentioned, inflection points can completely change the meaning of a sentence.
  » Cadence
    › Does it vary?
    › Not too fast; not too slow.

- Pause
  - » Do you start your speech with one? Many professionals do – observe them.
  - » Are they in the right places; i.e., giving the audience time to absorb information or humor?

Use a **Video Recorder**

- Your skills will jump *exponentially* compared to the time you put into this exercise.
- It may be tough to watch, but you do want to improve, don't you?
- Set up a system to film yourself over and over. You don't need to do this in a professional studio. There are inexpensive camcorders available that do a good enough job. The important thing is that *you do it and review it* each time.
- Look for distracting mannerisms: hands in pockets, leaning, fidgeting, fig leaf position, etc.
- What messages do you send the audience, verbally and non-verbally?
- Is your total presentation in sync?
- Do you look professional?
  - » Appearance
  - » Personal grooming

Use a **Mirror**

- It's not as good as video, but a good idea, and *mandatory* before *all* presentations. (Think: messed up hair, food in teeth, stained shirt, etc.)
- Standing in front of a full length mirror gives you the opportunity to make corrections *immediately*.

- Check your smile, your posture, how you use your hands, and the other **Nonverbal** elements of communication.
- It's a good opportunity to practice specific gestures.

Use **Friends and Family** (If they'll let you!)
- My favorite way is to practice my speech with my wife while driving down the highway at 60 miles per hour! Talk about a *captive* audience (*her* words, not mine)!

Use the Support of a **Toastmasters Club**
- One of the *best* places to practice!
- One of the most important parts of the meeting is the **Evaluation of Speeches**, where besides reviewing what the speaker did *well*; a few *areas for improvement* are also suggested.
- A goal of a Toastmasters Club is to encourage, and help members continually improve their speaking.
  » Keep in mind: this is a very forgiving audience that *wants* you to succeed. They'll purposely give you their undivided attention and are far more forgiving of any foibles than a *real* audience.
  » This is also one of the best places to practice **Answering Questions**
  » Taking on this part of your talk with a forgiving audience will pay enormous dividends. You might even want to plant some of the tougher questions you might get asked.

Speak at **Other Venues**.

- Chambers of Commerce, Social Clubs, and Church Groups are places to get responses from different, and often more critical, audiences.
  - » It's not Toastmasters, where there is a formal Evaluation part of the meeting. You'll have to take their temperature through their body language, eye contact, facial expressions and questions.

Use the Wisdom of your **Mind's Eye** - one of my favorites!

- For me, this works especially well for me when power walking. Getting my endorphins going helps the creative process. I go over parts of an upcoming talk and often think of ways to improve it. I carry a small digital recorder so I don't forget once my walk is over.
- Some do this visualization before falling asleep and say this imprints the presentation in their mind. Others meditate upon waking, before they get out of bed.
- **Visualization** is a powerful tool.
  - » One of my favorite examples of this was an American POW who played golf in his mind every day he was in prison. After he was released and returned to the states and played his first real round of golf in years—*he achieved his best score ever*!
  - » I remember this story about Winston Churchill:
    His driver had just opened the door at the entrance to a place where Sir Winston was to speak. The prime minister appeared deep in thought and didn't budge from his position. After holding the door for quite a while, the

chauffeur cleared his throat and asked, "Sir, are you OK? Is anything wrong?" Mr. Churchill calmly replied, "No, my dear man. I am just working on my *impromptu remarks!*" If one of the greatest orators of all time believed in practicing this way, we can use that technique, also.

Practice out loud even if you're the only one who will hear you!
- **Read out loud and *Hear* the difference!**
- This is really great for strengthening your voice and hearing how you sound to yourself.
- Pick a variety of material to read.
  - » Read aloud several news headlines and the stories that follow.
  - » Read magazine articles.
  - » Read children's books
    - › These are among the best to read, since many are written with the intention to be read aloud to kids.
    - › If you have a child, or children to practice on, so much the better.
- Practice *all* the verbal elements of communication.
- Hearing yourself as you speak, and listening to a recording of yourself, are two of the quickest ways to improve your **Verbal Delivery**. Areas for improvement are quickly heard and usually easy to correct. Pay attention to your:
  - » **Pronunciation** and **Enunciation**
    - › Are words pronounced as they should be with the correct syllables emphasized?
    - › Is your diction correct, or are you mumbling?
    - › Are you speaking clearly and distinctly?

> If English is your second language, or if you have a regional accent, don't completely trust your own judgment on this, get the opinion of a trusted adviser.

» **Projection** of your voice
  > Will the entire audience be able to hear you clearly?
  > Is the projection consistent, or does your voice sometimes fade?

» **Inflection**
  > Do you speak in a boring monotone, or do you correctly put inflection into sentences that paint vivid pictures in the minds of the audience?

» **Cadence**
  > Is the pace of your delivery boringly the same, or do you quicken and slow down the speed based on emotion and content?

» **Pauses**
  > Do you stop speaking long enough for the audience to digest the words you've just spoken, or enjoy laughing at a humorous statement?

I know I just wrote about practicing in your mind's eye, and my next bullet point is to practice out loud. They're both important, and here's a personal story explaining *why*:

I remember practicing in my mind while preparing to talk at a memorial service for a friend who died much too young. I believed I had some important things to say and practiced the talk several times this way.

I thought I'd better try it out loud and started speaking. I couldn't get through it! I hadn't anticipated the emotional effect delivering that speech would have on me. WOW! Luckily, I started this practice several hours before the service, and had time to practice out loud a number of times. I also realized how important this friend had been to me and wanted to express my feelings to his friends and family.

These thoughts, plus the practicing paid off. My friend's brother called the next day and expressed, very emotionally, how meaningful my comments had been. My goal, because of the out loud practicing, was accomplished.

Lesson: Practice - Practice - Practice, and do it in *many* ways!

Deliver *Your* Speech

This is *your* time.

This is the time to present the speech you have developed, redeveloped, and possibly *re-re*-developed.

It's the speech you have practiced and practiced and practiced. You *are* prepared.

You *know* you will make the audience rock!

Remember to arrive early. Check all the things mentioned in the Venue Checklist and Meet & Greet the people who will be in attendance. It is less stressful to talk to people you've already met.

You've reviewed, and *re*-reviewed, your introduction with the person who will be presenting you. They will have the audience primed and ready for the great talk you'll be delivering.

Have your Mind Map, speech outline, or note cards (make sure to number them, in case they are dropped) with you, or at the lectern. (Maybe both, if you're a little paranoid.)

The Master of Ceremonies will complete his or her introduction of you and lead the audience in applause as you walk to shake hands. Then take your place on your mark, a preset spot on the stage, or at the lectern.

Before uttering your first word, find that friendly face of the person you met earlier in the audience and make eye contact. (If you can't find that person, make eye contact with another friendly face. There really are many out there!)

Take a deep breath.

Pause . . . till it's almost uncomfortable.

Start your presentation with your Opening Statement, and *Grab their attention!*

Things to remember:

- The audience *wants* you to be successful in your presentation.
  - » Usually, they are attending because they came to learn something.
- The title of your talk, and the introduction by the Master of Ceremonies, said *you* are the *right* person, at the *right* time, to be delivering *this* message.
- *Most* of the people watching and listening are glad it is *you*, and not *them* at the lectern delivering the talk.
  - » Many of them have a Fear of Public Speaking. They see you as an Expert.
- *Continuously* check the facial expressions and body language of your audience to be certain they are **Getting It!**
- Occasionally stop and ask, "Does that make sense?" or, "Am I making myself clear about this?"
- If you sense they're *not* **Getting It!**, rephrase your point. You can also give a different example or story that reinforces your message.
- *Never* apologize for . . .
  - » Not being 100% prepared.

- » Being nervous.
  - › If you bring up something like that, the audience will be looking for it, and the non-preparedness or nervousness will become a self-fulfilling prophecy.
- Make sure there is a glass or bottle of *room temperature* water nearby should you need it.
- Have your Mind Map or notes at hand. There's no disgrace in glancing at them to make sure you're on track and don't miss anything.
- If you are confident in your competence, the audience will sense this by the tonality of your voice and your body language.

As stated earlier, in your **Opening**, you tell them what you're going to tell them.

In the **Body** of your speech, you'll cover three to five main points and use the formula: Make a Point – Tell a Story for each of your points.

It's *your* speech, and you use *your* personal stories, connecting on an *emotional* level with your audience.

Once you've completed the body of your speech, it's time for the **Closing**.

- **Tell them what you told them.**
  - » Review the main points of your presentation. These are the ones, should someone be asked, that would answer the question, "What did you get out of his or her talk?"
  - » Repetition is one way to have your message sink in, so repeat those points you want the audience to take away with them.

- **Close strongly.**
  - » The *last* thing you say will most likely, be the *first* thing your audience will remember.
  - » Make this a challenge, motivational quote, or call to action. Deliver it *powerfully*.

Tips to Help the Audience GET IT!

As stated in the Foreword, the primary goal of all communications, verbal, written, or visual, is for the recipient(s) to **GET IT!**

Again, they don't have to agree with everything stated, but unless they **GET IT!,** there cannot be a meaningful discourse going forward.

Here are a few things that will help accomplish that goal:

The Law of Primacy and Recency

For any presentation, people will better recall the **first** and **last** things you say; It is human nature, and extremely relevant to public speaking.

This is why a *Strong* **Opening** and *Strong* **Closing** are so important. This is *not optional.*

The **Closing,** because of the recency effect, will carry slightly more weight than the **Opening.** The words and the delivery of the words in your **Closing,** should be *outstanding!*

Because of the **primacy effect,** it is *extremely* important that information is presented correctly the first time. The *first thing* *presented* makes a huge impression that, if incorrect, is often hard to override. There's only one chance to make a first impression!

Check and double-check that your opening statements are true and on message. Make certain that your quoted dates, statistics, quotes, news items, and other facts are true and verifiable. Ensure that information is the latest available. (Not a bad idea to Google those things a few days or less before delivering your presentation.)

If what you state in your opening is not correct, and you correct it later in your talk, many people will still remember your first statement.

Remember: Your Introduction, delivered masterfully by the Master of Ceremonies, has primed them for your opening. Use this momentum to *Grab* the audience's attention!

At the other end of the speech, we've all experienced excellent talks that ended *underwhelmingly* with a "Thanks for having me!"

Don't end *your* speech that way.

It's the equivalent of having a great meal and leaving room for dessert, then *seeing* a mouthwatering cheesecake covered with fresh strawberries on the dessert tray – and not being offered any! Bummer!

Do not underestimate the importance of this.

Lincoln's closing of the Gettysburg address is a great example:

"...from these honored dead we take increased devotion to that cause for which they gave the last full measure of devotion, that we here highly resolve that these dead shall not have died in vain, that this nation, under God, shall have a new birth of freedom, and that government *of the people, by the people, for the people, shall not perish from the earth."*

Write and rewrite, and rewrite again, the **Opening** and **Closing** of your speech, giving more attention to them than anything in the body.

Memorize them and practice, practice, practice them!

Practice your **Opening** and **Closing** *almost* ad nauseam!

PERSONAL STORY

Years ago I was working on a speech about using props in a speech and how, if used correctly, they could take a speech to the proverbial *next level.*

I was practicing the **Closing** of a speech with the challenging statement being, "Wouldn't it be a shame if you didn't take one more step and make that *good* speech - a *great* one!"

Following the advice of experts, I was practicing aloud, and experimenting by putting the **Inflection** on different words in the sentence, as well as varying the length of the **Pause**, and so on.

My daughter, Emily, obviously thought it was *too* much practice as she began pacing (as I sometimes do when practicing) and rephrasing my statements and saying, "*Wouldn't* it be a shame, Wouldn't it *be* a shame, Wouldn't it be a shame if dad *didn't* practice closing this speech one more time!"

As the saying goes, "You only have one chance to make a first impression" (you read that advice before!), which is a good segue to the next tip – **Repetition.**

Repeat – Repeat – Repeat

Repeating your message with slightly different language but the same core meaning is OK. It is *mandatory* if you want your audience to **GET IT!** Using a slightly different way of presenting the same meaning might be the ticket!

Repetition enhances learning. It's one of the ways your brain processes information and puts it into the memory bank. Even when watching a great presentation, people's minds naturally wander. Attention spans can be very short.

Throughout this book I have named the components, parts, and elements of a speech several times. Some of them, *more* than several times. I didn't do this by accident!

Think about **Repetition** as walking through high grass. The first time you walk through, look back, and you'll see a slight outline where you just walked. Tramp back and forth through the same grass several times, and gradually you'll wear a path. **GET IT?**

Continually check your audience to see whether they're absorbing and understanding your message. Their facial expressions and body language will, if you're monitoring them, tell you how well you're communicating.

It's also a good idea to – Ask!

Question the audience with language like, "Does that make sense?" and "Am I making this point clear?"

After asking - Pause. *Look* and *listen*. What does their nonverbal communication tell you? Remember: nonverbal trumps verbal! If you don't think they're **Getting It!**, rephrase your point and check, again.

Doing this throughout your presentation will definitely increase the audience's understanding and retention of your message.

I know. I know. I wrote this bit about checking the audience's reception of your message previously. Repetition – Repetition – Repetition!

Do Something Unusual

Another technique for getting your audience to remember your message is to **Do Something Unusual**.

Delivering something unexpected usually catches the attention quicker, and is remembered longer, than the same-old, same-old.

Something unusual might be the handling of a prop, a unique series of gestures, or even wearing a costume or uniform to emphasize something.

An albino squirrel or a two-headed snake will catch and hold, your attention, won't it?

Your something unusual must be related to your topic.

Doing something unusual, for unusual's sake and to be remembered, is not appropriate. It might take away from your message.

Bad Example

Wearing a wild colored suit, with tie, and shoes to match doesn't match with a presentation about caring for the elderly. Anything that disconnects from your main message should be avoided.

Good Example

When I was in Toastmasters, one of the members was a management consultant and gave a speech about labor and management negotiations.

He wore a double-brimmed baseball cap. Half the hat, from the top through the brim, was white, indicating management. The other half was blue, representing labor.

When he was speaking for management, the white side faced forward. For labor, it was the blue side.

The **Delivery** was enhanced by changing the style of presentation; **Words, Inflection, Posture**, and **Body Movement**, depending on his emphasis at the time - management or labor.

It was more than 30 years ago that I was in the audience for this speech; yet, *I still recall it.*

If you want them to remember - Do *Something Unusual!*

So, to repeat (following my own advice) if you want to increase the probability that your audience will remember your speech, include the following techniques:

• Primacy and Recency
• Repetition
• Something Unusual

Additional Speaking/ Presentation Tips

Visuals

Visuals help the audience **GET IT!** quicker, and retain it longer.

Remember, people learn differently. A very visual learner will really appreciate and benefit from the use of visuals. So will someone who is primarily an auditory or kinesthetic learner. There has to be a good balance between visuals and the speaker's presentation *without* the added **Visuals**.

One technique is to use the **Visual** – then either turn it off or put it away. This puts the visual out of sight and makes it clear to the audience that *you* are the center of your speech!

PowerPoint and Projected Media

YOU supply the TEXT!

If I project a slide showing a door ajar with a lighted EXIT sign above it, onto a screen, and simultaneously say, "It's time for you to leave!" – You **GET IT!**

The slide is clean and simple. *My* words supply the text. This keeps the slide, and hence the message, clean and simple!

There is no need to have text, stating what I just said, flying, dropping, or twisting in from one, two or more angles! This only confuses the audience. It truly lessens the understanding.

YOU are the star of your presentation - *Not* the slides!

PowerPoint, Keynote, and other **computer programs** can add to a presentation because people learn differently and *seeing* the message often leads to better understanding. Be careful though, because these tools can also *become* the presentation, making *your presence* almost unnecessary!

The technology today is so cool and easy to do that we're tempted to believe fancier and flashier is better. – *It's not!*

It has been, at least for me, extremely tempting to use every fancy build-in, build-out, and cool transition offered in today's PowerPoint/Keynote software programs. I love that stuff!

Always wanting, but knowing it's not best to use the latest in creative tools has been a challenge. I've sometimes felt addicted to incorporating all the bells and whistles available in these programs. (I probably should buy the first edition of these programs and trash all the updates and upgrades!)

I've spent more time than I'll admit building presentations that I thought, smoked! Once the presentation was developed, I made the observation - occasionally, I wasn't needed! Everything I should have been saying was bullet-pointed or written on the screen! Sometimes, it was almost like showing a silent movie to the audience. It wasn't always a movie that everyone would understand.

Also, because it was only text and graphics, it didn't communicate to people who are auditory learners. For the visual learners, it was much *too* much on the screen, and didn't deliver my message well.

Sensing I was doing something wrong, I began researching PowerPoint/Keynote Presentations. I read articles and spoke with people skilled in this field. *Presentation Zen* by Garr Reynolds, and a Slideshare.com presentation, *The Presentation Secrets of Steve Jobs*, by Carmine Gallo, were great resources.

Our minds can only focus well on one thing at a time. When we are looking at a screen, we see the image. If there's text on the screen, we see, and try to process that, also. (One opinion is we see the text on the screen as images.) Add the presenter's voice to this equation, and something will get missed, disconnected, or misunderstood.

The text on the screen does *not* reinforce the message - it competes, confuses, and *complicates* it!

Text is OK to have in your Presenter Notes. Printing them and using them as handouts *after* you present is acceptable. The text notes will reinforce the visual and auditory presentation you delivered.

For examples, look at some television commercials. Is everything the spokesperson saying already superimposed on the pictures, moving or still, you are viewing? Unlikely.

As you develop any visual presentation, the main thing to remember is: Keep it SIMPLE!

A few **Rules of the Road for PowerPoint/Keynote** are:

Without fail, have a **Plan B, and probably a Plan C**
- Stuff Happens.
- A bulb burns out, and you don't have a spare.
- You forgot the adapter to the projector.
- It just stops working!

Make certain you can give your presentation *without* the visuals.
- You could have flip charts as a backup plan.
- A whiteboard could help if you can draw quickly and well.

Have at least two copies of your presentation printed.

Print the presentation in the light table view.
- This will put all your slides on as few as one or two pages. (I like to take it a step further and laminate them. Just in case!)

Don't read your slides.
- The audience can do this, also.
- Rather than reinforcing your message, if the audience reads it as you are reading it, *less* information will be conveyed. They're probably reading at a different rate, and a disconnect occurs.

Have the slide *supplement* not be your presentation.
- Guy Kawasaki, the ex-Apple guru suggests a maximum of 10 slides in a 20 minute presentation.
- Make one point per slide.

- Limit fancy transitions, and make them similar between all slides.
- If you have a choice of 3D slides or 2D - make them 2D.
- Instead of a multicolored background, make it one color, perhaps with shading.
- Simple and cleaner is much better than fancy and cluttered.

Use Graphics

- Usually, make them high quality photos. istockphoto.com is a great site for finding and buying them.
  - » To make a point, keep them large and use very few per slide.
  - » Sometimes the graphic can take up the entire slide.
  - » **Important**: Graphics can be interpreted differently. The meaning one person might have could be dramatically different form another viewer's response.
  - » Think about the Rorschach test, commonly known as the inkblot test, used by the psychiatric world to help determine a person's mental state.
  - » Test and retest the meaning of graphics with others before using to avoid someone giving a meaning to the graphic different from your intention.
- Make sure any text can be read.
  - » Use simple fonts: Helvetica, Ariel, and Gill Sans.
  - » Guy Kawasaki, the ex-Apple guru likes Arial and suggests a point size of 32.
  - » Garr Reynolds likes the Gill Sans font.
- Use the **B Button** when a slide is no longer needed. The **B Button** blanks the screen.

» If you use a remote control, buy one that has a **B Button.**
» This immediately takes the attention *off* the screen, and puts it on *you*, the speaker. This is where the attention *should be!*

- Leave the room lights on.
  » Today's projectors are bright enough to allow this with no compromise in the quality of the projected image.
  » Even if your projector is not the latest in brightness, you're still best to leave the light on.
  » Darkness induces sleep. Worse, it puts all the focus on the screen. The audience should be looking at YOU. (Remember the **B Button!**)

Here's your takeaway from this discussion of Power Point/Keynote: The best way to get your message across, in *all* communications, is to keep it **S-I-M-P-L-E** and **C-L-E-A-N!**

Props

Props include visuals other than computer generated ones.

Again, because **Visuals** can enhance a speech, they can be another arrow in your quiver for presentations.

Here is a speech I delivered to my Toastmasters club that will show how props can be used effectively.

The initial speech Toastmasters ask members to give is called the Icebreaker. The purpose is to tell the club something personal about yourself to help them get to know you better.

My Icebreaker Speech was titled, The Hat Speech. What follows are some excerpts and explanations from that presentation.

"In our business, personal, and family lives, we all wear many hats.

"For instance, I wear the hat of a father, a son, a speaker, and, like all of you - *many* other hats.

"I thought a good way to let you know something about me and some of the hats *I* wear would be to *show* you those hats and give an explanation of *why* that hat fits *me!*

"I was born a *l-o-n-g* time ago in the bright spring month of April.

"To keep the sun out of my eyes, my thoughtful mother bought a hat for me."

I reach into a trunk I've pre-positioned next to me, and pull out a bonnet that looks as if it came out of the cowboy wagon train days.

After placing it on my head, and looking utterly ridiculous, I tell the audience, "I may look funny wearing this, but it *did* its job!"

I then take the bonnet off and place it on the nearest straight-laced man's head (I don't want to mess up a woman's hair!) and ask him to stand up and face the audience. He, of course, always looks as silly as I did, and the speech is off and rolling!

I won't replay the whole talk for you, but a few more examples will demonstrate further the use of props, audience participation, and humor.

At one point I place a two-foot high dunce cap on my head, and rhetorically ask, "Who knows what this is?

A dunce cap!" I announce quickly, while the audience is thinking hard about where I am taking them with this visual. I then continue, "By now you've figured out I'm not the sharpest knife in the drawer.

"I did, however, graduate in the *top 100 percent of my class!* (I pause here, because it's my sharpness test. Did *you* **GET IT?***)*

"If you have a teenager in the house, you'll understand the reasoning behind this cap. I didn't turn *stupid* till my first child turned *teenager!*

"I see some heads nodding.

"*You* know what I mean!

"*They* know *everything*, don't they!

"For those of you who haven't had the experience yet – *brace yourselves!*

"Who appreciates what I'm saying and wants to wear *this* cap?" I then hand it to one of the people raising their hand.

"The final hat I'll tell you about is a pink crown with gaudy glitter and designs on it." (They'll remember something *unusual*, won't they?)

After placing it on my head and waiting for the laughter and snickers to die down, I say, "We've all heard that expression. A man's home is his castle, right?

"I pretty much think that's true.

"But I don't want anyone to misunderstand me. *My* throne is the same place each one of *yours* is - Right between the bathtub and the sink!

"Who wants to wear the crown?" I ask.

And so the speech goes . . .

Props don't have to be so elaborate.

I once saw a person give a speech with a prop they *never used.*

Setting the stage for this speech, the speaker was a participant in a Toastmasters Speechcraft class. Speechcraft is a set number of classes that focuses each week on one aspect of public speaking.

The assignment for this class was – **Props!**

The speaker had been in the advertising business and took a very large portfolio case to the stage with him.

As he steadied the case, and occasionally shifted its position, he spoke about different ad campaigns his firm had completed for clients.

He presented details about the adverting business and told several stories that helped make his points.

It was a very interesting and informative speech, and the audience kept waiting to see pictures of the products and services he was discussing.

As the talk continued, anticipation grew, – and grew, – and grew!

After the allotted time – he closed his speech, stepped from behind the lectern with his *unopened* case in hand, and took his seat.

Suddenly, we all realized *how well he had used this prop!*

He didn't just *have* our attention for his ten-minute speech – he *captured* it and *held it*. The attention increased exponentially with each passing moment that he *didn't open the case.*

The effect of the case on the audience was planned and was one of the most effective uses of props I've ever seen.

(As expected, half of us wanted to grab that portfolio case and rip it open!)

A few rules about Props:

» Use them sparingly.
» Too many, and they take over the speech.

- Once used, put them away.
  - » If not put away, they become a distraction to your audience. (Remember the B Button in a PowerPoint presentation!)
- Practice with your prop(s)
  - » I've seen good presentations go bad because the use of a prop didn't work the way the presenter intended. (Think about a malfunction in a PowerPoint Presentation!)
- Make them appropriate to the speech.
- *Everything*, remember, should be in sync.
- We don't want the audience saying, "I *don't* **GET IT!**"

One last salient point about **Props**: The best one may be - *None!*

Example:

If I were to take a coffee cup and place it on the lectern and announce that my speech today will be about coffee, the audience will immediately fix their gaze on the prop cup and listen to my talk.

However, if instead of placing that cup on the lectern, I say, "Picture *your favorite* coffee cup!"

Now, I've *personalized* the speech, and for each of us who has a special person or memory attached to a coffee cup - we **GET IT!** Anyone who has one of those picture mugs or a *World's Best Daddy!* coffee cup or one from a souvenir shop from a favorite vacation, knows what I mean.

In *my* case, it's a thick, beige porcelain cup with a fading picture of the diner, Goody-Goody, on it. This diner was established in 1948 and is a St. Louis landmark. The owner, Richard Connelly, gave it to me on one of our many breakfast meals there. I love the restaurant and always make that association when I drink from that great mug.

You undoubtedly pictured an entirely different cup, one, I assume, with its own unique story connected to it.

The point is this: *Personalizing* a prop, *without showing it*, can be extremely effective.

Buzz Words

Another important tip, often overlooked is: **NO Buzz Words!**

I mentioned this earlier (remember *repetition*), but it bears noting again.

Buzz Words, or Jargon are usually specific to a particular industry. Often, we think of the tech industry or legal or medical professions having buzz words, acronyms, and jargon that many nonmembers of those groups can't understand.

Many occupations, generations of people, industries, clubs, geographical areas, etc., use words when speaking with each other that outsiders often don't understand.

When these words are used in a speech to outsiders the message can be hard to understand, and sometimes misinterpreted or lost. If people have trouble understanding your message, they'll give up trying and won't **GET IT!**

One of the ideas discussed in the Sandler Sales Course is that people don't like to feel *Not OK*. *Not OK* means you're not in your comfort zone. You don't understand what you're seeing and/or hearing. It's not an emotion we embrace. I know *I* don't like to feel *Not OK* and I imagine *you* don't either.

The problem with **Buzz Words** and other language we don't understand is that it makes us feel *Not OK*.

If either the message or the messenger makes us feel *Not OK* we'll soon tune them out. Their message will *not* be received, and we'll *never* **GET IT!**

This advice should be applied to the words you use with your audience.

Always consider the education and experience level of the people you're talking to. *Don't* talk above or try to impress with the words you know. You *won't* impress your audience - you'll *lose* them!

Using words, phrases, and ideas that your audience does not easily grasp is like placing a roadblock in front of them as they journey along with you as you deliver your speech. When this occurs they either have to figure out the meaning of what was said, or skip it and try to catch up to the speaker. A couple of these bumps in the road, and they'll give up and never **GET IT!**

There was a member of my Toastmasters Club who probably *forgot* more words than I *know*. I'm sure he gave great speeches, but, for the reasons just stated, I didn't **Get** all of them. I'm probably not the only person who felt a little bit *Not OK* each time he spoke.

If you're speaking with smaller groups of people and you think this might be a problem, early in your talk you can say, "I have a bad habit of using buzz words and jargon from my industry. I know I shouldn't, and I try not to. However, I do slip up sometimes and will greatly appreciate it if one of you will *please* raise your hand and stop me and ask what I mean if I fall into that mode. Will you do that for me? Please!"

That may help, but it won't work as well in large audiences.

Monitor the body language and facial expressions of your audience to see whether they are **Getting** your message.

Bottom line: check and recheck the words you use.

While we're talking about word choice and language, there's an old adage that says, "If you can't say it in front of your wife, mother, and daughter – *don't*." Keep that in mind for *everything* from your **Opening** through your **Closing.**

Handouts

Now, here's a tip about **Handouts** – *don't* hand them out!

A speech is best presented with **no distractions in the hands of the audience.**

Early handouts eliminate surprise! People will thumb through them and distract others.

More to the point, unless your materials contain information the audience needs *during* your presentation, wait until the end of your speech to distribute them.

Material containing information the audience needs during the presentation includes things like workbooks or manuals with diagrams and instructions needing supplementary notes added to the printed material.

Handing out other material at any other time will have people *reading* while you're presenting - *not* a good thing. It will probably *lessen* their understanding of your presentation. They will most likely not be following along with you, but either jumping ahead of your presentation or going back to review something in it. The reinforcement you might think you're providing by handing out your presentation *before* the presentation, will best occur *after* your speech. What you've presented will have had time to sink in. Reviewing is best done once away from the original talk.

Often, you can even save them the time and energy of taking notes by telling them that the information in your presentation is available online at your website. (If, of course, it is.)

Here are the options:
- Direct them to your site (it *is* on your business card and the flyer that informed attendees about your talk, correct?)
- Have them register to receive the white paper that summarizes and gives the highlights of your speech.
  - » This easily captures their email addresses for future email marketing activities you might want to conduct.
- Collect their business cards and email the white paper or presentation you promised.
- The email addresses may be available through the organizer of the event, and you can electronically send them to all attendees.

A big benefit is that these people have opted in to receive future emails from you. An opted-in email campaign will bring far better results than one that just grabs emails off websites. Spam filters will block many unsolicited emails, and people are less likely to open emails from individuals they don't know and don't have a relationship with. Email marketing, when done correctly, can be an extremely effective tool for selling products and services.

Don't hand out stuff just for the sake of handing out something. (Although do have plenty of business cards available.)

Be sure what your audience takes away is something that reinforces your message (there's that *repetition* thing, again) and has value. Too much *stuff* that is other than the message you delivered could make them feel baited and switched.

My handout, if distributed *after* a *No Sweat* Public Speaking! presentation, is a trifold brochure that contains a Mind Map of the NSPS formula.

It also lists the services I offer, and has all my contact information, including my email address, and website address.

A Special Offer and/or Call to Action can be added to a handout, enhancing its value as a marketing tool.

It's probably not a bad idea to have a business card attached to each handout piece. The odds of people keeping your card are much higher than keeping your brochure or flyer. Also, as more people scan business cards into their address books, the likelihood of a participant taking your card with them increases.

Humor

Humor can be a great addition to a speech.

Some see it as the icing on the cake of an already good presentation.

It can put the audience *and* the presenter at ease.

Humor can also, if appropriate, put a needed laugh into an otherwise serious talk.

That's the *good* news.

The *bad* news about humor - it's *tough*.

For *some* people – *really* tough!

Even *more* bad news is that if your audience isn't laughing *with* you, they might be laughing *at* you. That's not a good thing, either!

Some people are naturally humorous and seem to easily make humor a part of their speech and *do it successfully.*

Others could have writers from Jay Leno, David Letterman, and Jerry Seinfeld TV shows writing their lines and never even receive a *smile* from an audience.

Successful humor depends upon:
- Great, and *appropriate,* material that's timely and relevant to the presentation and audience
- Timing
- Effective use of the pause
- Mastery of inflection
- Facial expressions
- Gestures
- *Lots* and *lots and lots* of practice
- The ability to get back on your feet *after* you've laid an egg (Take it from *my* experiences, you *will!*)

Don't expect every humorous story to get roaring laughter.

Don't make others the brunt of your humor. Mock yourself. Use self-effacing humor. Tell the audience about *your* foibles and misadventures.

I've made the mistake of poking fun of my wife's cooking. First, it wasn't true. She's a magnificent cook. Second, it was not correct, and the dagger stares from the audience quickly delivered that message!

Now, I tell about *my* efforts as a chef. Like the time my son, after starting to eat a meal I had prepared said, "Dad, what's in this? (Pause) *They may ask me in the Emergency Room!*"

Even the pros - those mentioned above and the late, great Johnny Carson and others - with the best writers and having practiced before a live audience, have bombed, bombed, and bombed again.

It's how you recover and move on that is important.

Also, unless you're specifically doing standup comedy, don't do a *shtick* (a comic theme or gimmick).

Some speakers think every speech should start with a joke, even if completely unrelated to their talk – Wrong! Seldom is telling a joke the way to open a speech. Open that way and *you* might become the joke!

A story with a punch line might be an appropriate opening. Be prepared that if it's not funny or gets only polite laughter, you might be starting negatively versus the positive opening that all speeches should have.

If humor is an area of your speaking that you want to improve, there are professionals who coach humor and whom may be worth seeking out and hiring.

Dry Mouth

Dry Mouth, or as some call it, **Cotton Mouth**, can be very frustrating and, obviously, lower the quality of your speech. There are a number of causes with nervousness being one of the leading contributors. Reducing anxiety can lessen a dry mouth. I'll address just how to in a moment.

Here are a few quick fixes for dry mouth:

Have *room temperature* water available.

- Iced water and hot drinks can have negative effects on the vocal chords.

- Take a sip when you need it. You'll be *Pausing* your talk, and that's probably a good thing. It will let the audience absorb, and think about, your message.

- To be certain you have it, *bring your own* bottle of water.
  - » I prefer a bottle with a cap, and bring my own. Better to have this fall off the lectern onto papers or the floor than a glass of water.
  - » Don't drink too much water. Having to take a bathroom break in the middle of a speech is not something you want to happen!

Place a lozenge (probably *not* cherry because it will give you a red tongue!) between your cheek and gum.

- Experiment with this *before* the speech, and have extras available.
  - » Too large a piece will be a distraction to you and the audience; too small, and it won't last long enough to do the job.

- Some say biting your lip will stimulate saliva. (Don't bite too hard or you *will* have a red mouth!)

Here are a few tips about avoiding dry mouth

- Avoid salty foods.

- Avoid drinks that contain alcohol or caffeine.
  - » Some commercial mouth rinses contain alcohol.

- Establish good oral hygiene habits.

- Some medications, prescription and nonprescription, cause a dry mouth. Check with your physician and read the warnings on the labels. Perhaps it's a medication you can take *after* your talk.

Before Speaking. . .

Don't drink soda, eat cabbage, or anything acidic, because you could wind up belching in front of your audience!

Don't starve yourself, either. A growling stomach, while probably not heard by others, will be a distraction to you.

Water is great, but not a lot.

Give yourself a good pep talk:

- "They will love me!"
- "I'm going to rock this audience!"

Read, Listen To, and Watch Videos of Great Speeches

Study how the masters do it.

- Martin Luther King – "I Have a Dream," 1963
- John F. Kennedy – Inaugural Address, "Ask Not What Your Country Can Do For You. Ask What You Can Do For Your Country," 1961
- Winston Churchill – "Iron Curtain," 1946
- Lyndon Johnson – "We Shall Overcome," 1965
- Franklin Roosevelt – Inaugural Address, "We Have Nothing to Fear but Fear Itself," 1933

There are some great sites online where these can be found. If a video, watch the nonverbal communication as you listen to the speech. For audio and video, list carefully for inflections, changes of cadence and pauses.

There are also professional motivational speakers who regularly tour the country. Try to attend some of their events. Being in a live audience will give you an opportunity to get the *total experience*. Be sure to look around to see whether the audience is reacting the way you are. If not, why not?

I've had the opportunity to see and hear Zig Ziglar, Les Brown, Brian Tracy, Denis Waitley, Wayne Dyer, Tony Robbins, and many more. *Nothing* compares with being in the audience for speakers of this caliber.

Be Certain the Audience is GETTING IT!

Everyone will not grasp your message in the same way simultaneously. It is important the audience **GETS IT!**

Constantly *Take Their Temperature!*

As I have stated several times throughout this book, the goal of all communication, verbal, written or visual is this; that the recipient(s) **GET IT!** as quickly as possible.

They may not agree with all our message. They may not agree with any of our message. They may be somewhere in the middle. Unless they **GET IT!,** we can't have a meaningful conversation going forward.

You won't know whether they're **GETTING IT** or not, unless you constantly monitor the reception of your message.

Here are several ways to *Take their Temperature.*

Look at Their Eyes

- If they are giving eye contact, they are paying attention to your talk and processing your message. This is a *good* sign! People need to be *active*, not passive, listeners.

Check Facial Expressions

- Confusion, neutrality, boredom, or enlightenment will come across fairly clearly.
- Nodding heads saying, "I agree" or heads indicating, "I don't agree" are *good* signs.
  - » These people are paying attention and comparing *your* message to *their* world.
- Yawning, snoring and drooling are *not* good signals from the audience!
  - » They could indicate a loss of sleep, but if too many are sending these signals, change something in your delivery - quickly!

Look at Body Language

- Leaning forward indicates attentiveness.
- Slouching is a sign they are not as engaged as the people leaning forward.
- Folded arms indicates defensiveness, but they *are* **Getting It!**

Ask your audience if they are Getting It!

- Often in my presentations, I'll ask the audience, "Does that make sense?"

» After asking, pause. Look into the crowd to receive your answer.

» Even take a question if you feel it's an opportunity to clarify something.

Important!

If you see someone is not **Getting** your message, it's usually best not to single out that individual.

This could embarrass them. That's not a good thing.

It's best to assume others aren't **Getting It!,** either. The correct course of action is to restate it. This will reinforce your message with those who *are* **Getting It!**, and increase the probability that others *will* **GET IT!**

Sometimes, things have to be repeated, and sometimes they have to be stated differently. Remember that people learn in different ways: audibly, visually, and kinesthetically. If possible, have your presentation address several of these learning styles.

Have a Specific Time set aside to Answer Questions

• You should tell the audience about this when delivering the **Opening** to Your Talk. The **Opening** is where you "Tell them what you're going to tell them."

• Telling *how* and *when* you will handle questions is part of this. The fact that you've set aside time for answering questions is important. It's part of the 'Up Front Contract' you have with your audience.

• Telling this in your **Opening** should eliminate or lessen hands that get raised during your talk from people who have questions.

» If hands still appear, remind them that you've set aside time for questions before the conclusion of your talk. Also, mention that many of their questions will be answered in the rest of your presentation.

This **Q&A Period** should *not* be at the end of your talk.

You want the **Closing** of your Speech to be powerful, and the possibility of ending a presentation with negative questions is avoided by taking them before the closing. The **Question and Answers** and **Closing** are two distinctive parts of the **Delivery** of your Presentation.

The **Bottom Line** is this: You want your audience to understand your message. Continually checking in with your audience throughout your presentation helps assure that they are **Getting It!** and prevents you from becoming a non-communicator. You certainly don't want to be that!

Join Toastmasters

Toastmasters is an International organization. Recent figures show they have a membership approaching 250,000 in more than 12,500 clubs in 106 countries.

One of the most valuable benefits of being a member is the nurturing environment where everyone truly wants to help the other members.

Toastmasters offers two tracks: speaking and leadership. Very specific skills are practiced, and there are degrees of competency that can be achieved. Both are excellent ways to learn and hone skills that will benefit you forever. The skills to speak in front of groups and lead meetings are tools needed along the career path of life.

A standard meeting agenda follows, although an individual club may tweak it to satisfy the needs objectives of its members.

TIME	ACTION
6:00	**PRESIDENT** • Calls the meeting to order • Brings up chapter news and concerns • Introduces the Toastmaster for the meeting
6:05	**TOASTMASTER OF THE MEETING** • Introduces people who have filled Roles (Ah-Counter, Timekeeper, etc.) • Gives Speaking Tip of the Day • Introduces the member who offers a helpful reminder or tip
6:10	**SPEAKERS** • Toastmaster introduces speakers, who deliver prepared speeches • Following the speeches, the Toastmaster introduces the Table Topics Master
6:40	**TABLE TOPICS MASTER** • Explains Table Topics and theme • Conducts the Table Topics session • Returns control to the Toastmaster • Toastmaster then introduces the General Evaluator

6:50	**GENERAL EVALUATOR**
	• Calls for reports from:
	  » Speech Evaluators
	  » Timekeeper
	  » "Ah," "Like," "You know" Counter
	• Following reports, General Evaluator makes general comments about the meeting and returns control to the Toastmaster
	TOASTMASTER
	• Thought of the Day
	  » Toastmaster introduces presenter who enthralls members with an inspiring thought or quotation.
	  » Following the Thought of the day, Toastmaster thanks everyone for coming and returns control to President.

6:55	**PRESIDENT** • Thanks any guests for coming • Asks for comments • Asks for volunteers for the following week's positions • Closing remarks
7:00	MEETING ADJOURNS

Credit for Agenda: Wellesley College Chapter of Toastmasters International

Created by: Carly Grisham and Carol Cross Wodtke

Usually, three to four prepared speeches are given at each meeting. The speakers have very specific goals for each speech. These goals are clearly stated in manuals distributed to each member. Objectives include: Working with Props, Use of Body Language, Vocal Variety, Persuading with Power, and others.

Most members consider the Evaluation portion of the meeting to be the most important part.

Each speaker's *speech* is evaluated based upon the assignment and the speaker's experience. (I emphasized *speech* because *that* is what is being evaluated - *not* the individual. There *is* a clear distinction, and it should always be remembered.)

The Evaluator reviews the Content and Delivery of the talk. The evaluator's remarks should follow the Sandwich Formula: Say something positive, point out something that needs improvement, and say something else positive.

Keep in mind, the evaluator's opinion is an opinion from *one person*.

Many clubs have forms that are handed out to the entire audience where space is available to give the speaker more opinions on their delivery and message. The same *Sandwich Formula* should be followed. The more specific comments members receive, the more likely they will improve, and that *is* the reason they joined Toastmasters!

Before joining a club, my suggestion is to visit at least three or four in your area. Each club has its own flavor. Some are very regimented and adhere to Robert's Rules of Order and are strict about the way things are done at meetings. You'll also find clubs at the other end of the spectrum, where things are a little loose. There are many between these extremes. Find the one where you feel most comfortable.

There are also company clubs within large corporations, and clubs specific to certain interests, such as humor or professional speaking. There are advantages and disadvantages to each. For instance, giving speeches in front of peers, bosses, and underlings in a company club is far different from giving talks in front of a non-company one.

Here's *my* story about why it's important to visit several clubs before joining:

Long ago, I thought being a public speaker would be something I might want to do someday. I've always been a big fan of Zig Ziglar, Brian Tracy, Tony Robbins, Les Brown, and other professional presenters.

The high school in my area was offering an adult educational course in Public Speaking. It was being presented by members of a local Toastmasters Club. I decided to sign up for the course.

The only person I told about this was my wife. I figured she had to know where I was going for a few hours once a week. Furthermore, if I decided to drop out, she would be one of few who would know, and I wouldn't have to explain my *failure* to others.

I enjoyed the course and learned a lot. Our final class was held at the instructor's Toastmasters Club where we got to observe a meeting and received our class completion certificates.

I decided to join this club.

My Ice Breaker Speech, the first manual speech where we tell the others about ourselves, went very well. My second speech bombed because of lack of preparation.

The members were very friendly and extremely smart. It was the smartness that turned out to be a non-fit for me. All the members must have belonged to Mensa, the genius club. There were too many discussions and speeches that left me scratching my head. (If you've read this far, you probably surmised that I graduated in the half of the class that made the top half possible!)

I dropped out, and stupidly, didn't immediately look for a different club. I guess I thought all Toastmasters clubs were like this one. Turns out, they're *not*. It wasn't until several years later that I ventured again, into a Toastmasters Meeting.

This one was close to home. Luckily, during the first meeting I attended, I knew this was the club for me. During the intermission, two members came up and introduced themselves. *Instantly,* these *new* people in my life were like *old* friends! I never looked at another club. Many are still friends today.

Great information, as well as a listing of Toastmasters clubs in your area, is available at www.toastmasters.org. Guests are always welcome so check the site and visit several clubs.

Speech Competition

Toastmasters, and other speaking clubs, sometimes have speech contests.

When I was a Toastie, I entered several competitions. I won a few, but lost more than I won. I hate to disagree with the famous quote from coach Vince Lombardi, but "Winning is *not* the only thing!"

It's really the *process*, not necessarily the event, that's most important.

In the club I belonged to, there were some amazing speakers. One member, Paul, had forgotten more words than I ever knew. Another speaker, Dan, had a great baritone voice that, had he been a preacher, would have sounded like God himself from the lectern. (My voice is fairly nondescript.)

Now, if I had decided not to speak when either of these people were participating in a contest, it would have been silly. First, as in any given contest, the presumed winner could stumble.

Second, it's the *journey*, not the *destination*, that is important.

I remember being a participant in a local National Speaker's Association (the leading professional association for speakers) Showcase Showdown. Each contestant was given exactly four minutes for their speech, including the introduction. This is an extremely short amount of time to get a message across. I got some great coaching from Kelly, a professional speaker and speech writer. Several times, she helped me look literally at five words in my talk and decided which three of them to use! (See the Rule of Three on page 194.)

I lost track of the number of hours I spent on that four-minute presentation. However, the process was more productive than I'm able to explain. That exercise taught me how important it is to get your message across quickly and succinctly.

I did not win that Showcase event, at least not in the traditional sense of winning.

My win was more about the journey. Participating in this contest was great reinforcement for the important fact that I needed to be reminded of and that is:

The only person you really need to compete with is – Yourself!

- I needed to give the best speech Fred Miller can give.
- I needed to give a speech that was better than the last one I gave.

- I needed to give a speech that improved one thing from previous speeches and the critiques I received on them.

Keep this lesson in mind the next time you think about not participating in a contest because you think the competition is better than you.

Enter the contest – *You immediately WIN!*

Filler Words

"Umms," "errs," "ahs," and phrases such as, "like," "you know," "and," etc. are used to fill dead air in a speech because the speaker either has a bad habit, is nervous, or both.

Such fillers can be extremely distracting. They are the physical equivalent of jingling change in your pockets, swaying back and forth, thumping your fingers on the lectern, or any other nervous habit.

In Toastmasters, we often had an "Ah" Counter who would ring a bell when someone used one of these fillers. Sometimes that kind of Pavlovian type of negative re-enforcement worked.

Unfortunately, some people have this habit, and have it *really* bad. It's very hard to break. If you do this, being aware of it is a huge step towards eliminating it. That's one of the reasons comments from trusted friends is so important. Listening to, and watching your own speeches, will let you know if you have this affliction.

The important thing is to be *aware* of the fillers. Stop talking, and *don't* fill the silence.

You *will* catch yourself about to use a filler, and you *will* reduce the fillers.

Remember that **Pausing** gives your audience time to digest your message. **Pausing** *enhances* the delivery of the content of your talk. You don't have to, nor should you, fill all the moments of your talk with words.

Don't use a filler – **P-A-U-S-E.**

Connect with Your Audience Emotionally

Some presentations are fairly cut and dried. Their purpose is to convey content. Nothing more and nothing less is expected.

Other presentations, perhaps ones you give or want to give, have a goal in mind that has a better chance of being achieved if you connect emotionally with your audience.

How deeply you engage the audience and deliver your speech will determine how well you connect *emotionally* with the audience. For many talks, you *do* want to make an emotional connection.

Delivering with passion and connecting on an emotional level will trump the perfect-language, non-emotional presenter every time.

Example

My good friend and internet mentor, Russ Henneberry, is an internet marketing expert.

He develops, and helps others develop: web sites, blogs, email marketing campaigns, social media campaigns, and many other things related to internet marketing. He *really* knows his stuff!

Russ holds a monthly MeetUp Meeting named, Tiny Businesses, Mighty Profits. He has established himself as an authority in this area.

Part of his marketing plan is to have people perceive him as an expert. The speaking he does at his MeetUps gives his audience that perception. They are so popular that people not signing up far in advance will likely not be able to attend because the room is filled with earlier registrants.

From the get-go, Russ connected with his audience on an emotional level.

At his first MeetUp, he announced we would go around the room and give everyone an opportunity to introduce themselves with their elevator speech. Russ then said, "I'll go first."

Here's what he said:

"I'm an entrepreneur, a teacher, a son, a father, a husband, and ... **I'm a Failure.**"

No one expected to hear those words. Everyone, though, could relate to them.

Russ then went on to explain about a business he had owned and that failed. He elaborated on all the mistakes he had made and how the business had drained him financially and emotionally.

When he uttered that phrase, "I'm a Failure" those words had the same effect on the attendees as when Renee Zelwicker exclaimed in the movie, Jerry McQuire, "You had me at "Hello!"

Everyone in Russ' audience *instantly* connected to him on an emotional level.

I cannot over emphasize the effect of that statement.

Too often we hear speakers talk about how great they are and their many accomplishments. They hardly ever mention failure, and so often, don't connect emotionally with their audiences.

Failure is part of life. We learn more from what goes wrong than what goes right. When something works the first time we try it, we usually don't stop and analyze why it worked. Failing stops us. And, if we're smart about it, we try to determine why success didn't occur. We may then, change something, and try, try again.

However, most speakers, and most people, don't like to admit their failures, especially in a public forum.

Russ seized the moment, grabbed his audience with his honesty and with that *pattern interrupt* phrase, **"I'm a Failure"** and has held them ever since!

Think how *you* can connect emotionally with *your* audience.

What *personal* stories will relate to points in the body of *your* presentations?

Emotional Presentation Tip

If your presentation is extremely personal and emotional, it's best to print it out in a large font, and *read* it.

Example: If you're called upon, or want to deliver eulogy for someone you have an emotional attachment to, *reading* it will help assure you complete the intended task.

The Rule of Three

Three blind mice.

The Three Stooges.

Three strikes - you're out!

Ready – Aim – Fire!

The third time is the charm.

The Father, the Son, and the Holy Ghost.

The number **Three**, throughout history and used in a variety of ways, has been important, and continues to be.

A Three-Act play is the standard structure in Hollywood.

In a speech, there is the Opening - Body - Conclusion.

When telling jokes, the formula is: Setup - Anticipation - Punch line.

If you want to emphasize a point and have people remember: Repeat - Repeat - Repeat.

For speakers, it's *essential* to study this, implement it, and become an expert at using it! (That was three, wasn't it?)

In his book, *Writing Tools: 50 Essential Strategies for Every Writer*, Roy Peter Clark provides insights to the magic of the number three: "The mojo of three offers a greater sense of completeness than four or more."

Clark correctly points out, "We use **one** for power. Use **two** for comparison, contrast. Use **three** for completeness, wholeness,

roundness. Use **four or more** to list, inventory, compile, and expand."
This is *great* advice. Understand it - Think about it when developing your talks - Use it!

The Parenthetical Statement

A parenthetical statement is a temporary departure from the main theme. It is a statement that, if you were reading it, would be in parentheses. In delivering your talk, you *speak that thought* to your audience. It can add a new dimension to your presentation.

It can be an extremely effective way to step out of your speech, make a specific point, and reinforce your connection with your audience.

For instance, I might be talking about hard work, then pause, and state, as if in parentheses: "Speaking of hard work, tonight's program would have never happened had it not been for Jackson Smith's untiring efforts and attention to detail."

Here's another example: "I went to an auction at the main post office the other day. Have you ever been to one of those events? All the weird stuff they auctioned was truly amazing. (Here's something else I found amazing – the large number of people who lowered their heads and put on dark glasses when the local TV station reporter and camera man came in to do a story!)"

Parenthetical statements can be enhanced by using body language that also indicates parentheses. Stepping to the side of your delivery position, placing a hand to the side of your face as if telling a secret, and bending slightly forward will get the attention of the audience and better convey the statement.

Now, stepping outside this writing, I want to tell you, "*This* can be *powerful!*" **GET IT?**

195

Speak Conversationally

Don't talk *at* your audience. Talk *to* them.

Talk to the audience as you would talk to an individual. *Don't talk to them like reading something you wrote!*

Unless you are delivering an academic paper to a very specific audience, keep your language simple.

Avoid buzz words, industry specific jargon, slang, and high-falutin' words made to impress people. You won't impress your audience with that kind of language; you'll *lose* them! The best words are short words that people immediately understand.

Using fewer words to get your point across is best. Just like the visuals you use, keep your speech s-i-m-p-l-e, clean and easily understood.

If your presentation makes technical or industry specific words needed, give the definitions of those words and phrases *as you're presenting them. Don't* assume all your audience knows the meaning. Often, a word or phrase can have several meanings and being specific in your definition helps clarify it even in the minds of those who are *in the know.*

Let your audience know up front that you welcome the show of a hand if at any point in the presentation they do not **Get It!**

Again, **a good speech should be like a one-on-one conversation**; the difference is that *you*, the speaker, are doing all the talking. You are, however, getting feedback by observing the audience's facial expressions and body language. Check those frequently to be sure your audience is **Getting It!**

The *Show Before the Show*

Have you ever gone to a live concert where a major super star is the headliner?

How many acts appeared *before* the super star came to the center of the stage?

There were probably several opening acts. Their purpose was to warm up the audience for the main attraction.

If you've ever been to a Cirque du Soleil show you've noticed cast members, walking thru the audience and performing, as guests enter. Those folks are also warming the audience up for the main event.

Speaking of main events, the championship fight is never the first match in the ring, is it? There's a definite reason. The promoter wants to build up excitement for the championship, and have all in attendance laser focused when the big bout occurs.

Sometimes, music can warm up the audience. I once attended a Motivational Rally where Tony Robbins was one of the featured speakers. Even before getting into the seating area attendees could hear Eye of the Tiger, the theme song from Rocky, blasting thru the arena. You could *feel* that song building energy and anticipation. When Tony jumped onto the stage, we were primed and ready - WOW!

If you're the first of several speakers, *you* could be warming the audience up for the next speakers.

If you are not the first speaker, the previous presenters could be warming the audience up for you - Good!

If you are the first, or only speaker, consider developing your own *Show Before the Show*.

You probably don't want to be the first speaker on the agenda if the audience has not been warmed up in some way. True, your Introduction, delivered professionally by the Master of Ceremonies, will accomplish much of this. However, if you want to add an extra level of anticipation and readiness, you'll want more than that. You want the audience in the right frame of mind, anticipating YOU. A *Show Before the Show* could be the answer.

Ideas

Make a PowerPoint Show with slides, and music that is relevant to your talk. Have it playing on a loop as the crowd arrives.
- For my signature speech, I have a loop of people with fear and nervousness on their face.
- The captions similar to: "They want *everyone* to come to the lectern and speak!" and "He's not walking over to *me* with that microphone, *is he?*"
- I have the theme song from the movie Jaws playing.
- This combination of slides and music sets the stage for my presentation.

Have music, related to your talk, playing as guests arrive.
- If your topic is baseball, Take Me Out to the Ballgame would do the job.

Like the Cirque Du Soleil cast members, walking thru the audience and performing, before the show, maybe something similar would fit your topic.
- A wandering magician, who walks thru the crowd making coins

and currency disappear, could be a fit for someone talking about personal finances, retirement and other money issues.

Don't speak with a *Cold* Audience. *Warm them up!*

Continually Hit the *Refresh* Button

One of the only things in life that's certain is – **Change**.

If you're not continually updating and changing your Introduction, Opening, The Body of your Speech, and Closing regularly, they will get stale and lose the impact they initially had.

Some of the information you're delivering may be old and out-of-date. That's not a good way to build trust and credibility with audiences!

Language evolves, also. Words that were on the mark when presented years ago, may now come across like a lady wearing a poodle skirt, saddle shoes and sporting a beehive hairdo. (Some of you will have to Google those items!)

There's a great site, www.wordspy.com, that posts new words and phrases, that is worth checking out now and then to keep your knowledge of verbiage current.

Even Keynote Signature Speeches need a makeover on occasion. The basic points you want to make won't change each time you do this, but the examples used to reinforce those messages should be made current with the present time.

For instance, if you were speaking about discount stores and gave examples using E.J. Korvette and Zayres, today's audiences might not have a clue what you're talking about. E.J. Korvette filed for bankruptcy in 1980 and the Zayre discount store chain closed in 1990. (Of course, those examples might be relevant if you were speaking about the demise of some of them.)

One way to keep on top of your subjects is to set up Google Alerts for key parts of your talks. Using examples from recent news stories helps connect with audiences and adds to your credibility as an expert on top of their subject.

Updating material is, like many things in life; a *Process* – not an *Event*. Approach this with the Japanese workplace philosophy Kaizen that focuses on making continuous small improvements which keep a business at the top of its field.

Have your radar up for ideas, events, new products, new procedures, news items, etc. that are relevant to your presentations and speech material. Following this philosophy is much better than making major redoes of your material every few years. (Think about someone asking to see pictures of your family. You pull out your wallet and show a picture of your son in a baby stroller. Cute pic, but he just graduated high school!)

Adopt the Yoga mantra of being *always present and in the moment*. Incorporate what you discover into your presentations, and you'll always keep that great material of yours - Fresh!

Brand Yourself with a Signature Closing

If you're a fan of Zig Ziglar, the famous motivational speaker from Yazoo City, Mississippi, you're familiar with his signature close: "And I will see *You* At the Top!"

This was the title of Zig's first book, and something he was always able to tie in with his speeches. Being both motivational and self-help in nature, this Signature Close made sense to his audiences.

It was always the final statement he used in closing all of his great speeches, and left the attendees feeling that, yes, they too, can *Make it to the Top!*

If you hear the phrase, "See you at the Top!" you think of Zig Ziglar. Great job of branding!

Walter Cronkite, the famous CBS anchorman always ended his nightly news casts with the his signature sign-off, "And that's the way it is!"

Another famous personality, of radio fame, was Paul Harvey. His branding close was, "Paul Harvey. . . Goooood Day!" Another branding phrase of his was, "The rest of the story."

The late Tim Russert's sign-off was: "That's all for today. We'll be back next week. If it's Sunday, it's *Meet the Press.*"

My friend Russ Henneberry named his enterprise, Tiny Business, Might Profits. When he closes his presentations, it goes like this: "*Tomorrow*, start using the tools and techniques we've discussed this evening. In a very short time *your* Tiny Business (pause) will have (pause) *Mighty Profits!*"

Isn't that great! Each presentation is ended by branding his company.

When I was in Toastmasters, and after delivering many speeches, I developed a signature close that incorporated the phrase:"*Challenge - and a Prediction.*" That phrase was easy to weave into the closing of a number of talks.

For instance, if my subject was using Props in the delivery of a speech, it went like this: "I'm going to close (Always tell your audience what you're going to do – then do it. The Close should *not* be a surprise!) with a *Challenge – and a Prediction.* My Challenge is this: The next time you prepare, practice, and deliver a speech, incorporate a prop or two into your delivery. Do *that*, and my prediction is *this*: *Your* speech will have a *far greater affect* on the audience!"

Now, My *Challenge and Prediction to you* is this: Develop a closing statement that brands you and your talks.

Do *that*, and my prediction is *this*: Your brand will grow and grow – making *you* the Go-To Person in your area of expertise!

Timing

Timing is extremely important and can be a challenge for some speakers.

When new Toastmaster members start their speaking journey, they are generally quite nervous. The effects of this anxiety can be seen when a five-minute speech is hurriedly delivered in three minutes or less. (For that speaker, though, it felt as if it lasted an eternity!)

At the other end of the spectrum are the presenters who go *on and on and on* with their presentation. This is not good.

Clean, simple and *shorter than expected* are the rules to follow. Usually, it is far better to take *less* than the time you are allotted for your presentation.

Better to have the audience wanting more of you than feel they've had too much!

It's crucial to have respect for the program you are speaking at, and for the time of other speakers. You certainly wouldn't want someone to continue to present into the time set aside for you, and should not do that to others.

The audience's time must also be respected. They have schedules to keep, and not delivering your material within the time they were expecting, is not acceptable.

Completing a talk too soon can prove troublesome. If you've practiced, as you always should, it could be you have left out important material. *Yikes!*

If you finished too soon, and said all you had to say, then you didn't plan and prepare well for the time set aside for your presentation.

Suppose the program had you down for one hour. Then, fifteen minutes after your Opening, you delivered your Closing! People who came to see and learn from you may feel cheated. You might also have thrown a ringer into the entire agenda.

The Timing Challenge can be lessened by good planning and practicing. Mind Mapping can be a good tool for adjusting your time *on the run* because of the modules you built when developing the talk.

I once spoke at a Toastmaster District Convention. Arriving early, I checked out the room and equipment, and had my *Show before the Show* on the screen, looking great. Less than ten minutes before I was scheduled to speak, the projector *stopped working!*

No one was able to revive it, and a spare projector had to be set up. Two of us were scheduled for about forty-five minutes each, but because of the projector problems, each had to cut the time of our speeches. Luckily, mine was in modules that were easily resized to fit the lesser time. Having practiced with the slides and a Mind Map made this much easier than if I had not been prepared for the unexpected.

If you're using PowerPoint or Keynote, consider using the Presenter Notes to show you the Elapsed Time or Real Time. Setting an alarm on your own watch for a five minute warning isn't a bad idea, either.

Always check, and double check, when first given the speaking opportunity, how much time you'll have to deliver your message. Recheck with the meeting planner the day before presenting and adjust your talk, accordingly.

Be *ahead* of time:
- Arrive *ahead* of time.
- Finish speaking *ahead* of time.

Customize

Always be **Audience Centered** in your presentations.

It's best to be *Specific* **Audience Centered.** Each audience is not the same.

This is why it's important, *well before* your presentation, to investigate and know:
- Who will attend?
- Why they are attending?
- What they are hoping to learn from your presentation?
- What is their current knowledge of your topic?
- What is their educational level? (If applicable.)
- What are their demographics? (If applicable.)
- Who, if anyone, is preceding you and following you?

When you have the answers to these questions, you can **Customize** parts of your presentation.

Customizing shows you did your research, care about your audience, and know your stuff.

Examples:

When I was in the coffee business, I recommended professional salesman and author, Jeffrey Gitomer to be the keynote speaker for our one of our national conventions. He got the gig and was outstanding.

One part of his presentation was a rant about the terrible coffee American Airways served. He told the story of calling them and complaining. They told him they had conducted taste tests and passengers loved their brew. Jeffrey went on to challenge them to put a coffee kiosk next to Starbucks in the Charlotte, North Carolina airport and see how well the product sold.

It was a great story, kept our attention, and was totally relevant to the audience - *Coffee People!*

I don't know whether Jeffrey even drinks coffee, but the fact that he told *that* story to a coffee convention showed us that he did his homework and customized it for his audience.

Unfortunately, all speakers, even well-paid professionals, don't always do this.

I recall sitting in a breakout at a convention where the speaker talked only about herself. It was so bad, the person I was sitting next to, wrote *Who Cares* at the top of a sheet of paper. We took turns putting hash marks every time she said something irrelevant to our industry. We filled the paper!

The **Meeting & Greeting** we discussed earlier can help with last minute customizing. Relating the story an attendee told before your presentation, naming individuals you greeted, and specifically mentioning companies and occupations goes a long way to connecting with an audience.

Your **Introduction**, specific to your audience, should be customized, also.

Example:
You've read my standard *Coffee Groaner* Introduction. When I rewrote this for a group of students who were writing books they hoped to have published one day, I included the following:

"Speaking with groups will be one of the BEST Ways to **promote *your* book**. If you present well, the perception will be that you are an expert and that you write well. Perception is reality."

That little bit of customization shows the audience you know something about them and their goals. You also will be presenting them with useful information to help them reach those dreams.

Deliver a Quotable Quote

Wouldn't you like to be the person who is quoted?

How cool would it be to have people repeating *your* words to others, and *crediting* you!

Well, coming up with that memorable line that people repeat is not as hard as it might seem.

Here are some tips to accomplishing this:

Google "quotable quotes."
* Read many of them so you have a benchmark of something to aim at.

Be clear and brief.

- It must be easily understood and easy to repeat.

Say it a bit differently than it's been said before.

- *Differently said* will be memorable.

Use metaphors.

- A metaphor is a figure of speech in which a word or phrase denoting one kind of object or idea is used for another to suggest a likeness or analogy between them.
- **Examples** (See if you can picture them in your mind's eye!):
  - » The *sun* was *smiling* on her.
  - » It's *raining cats and dogs.*
  - » He's *rolling in dough!*
  - » Tackle a large project the same way you would *eat an elephant* - one bite at a time.
  - » The *key* to collecting personal stories is to be, as they say in Yoga, "A person should always be present and in the moment."
  - » Capture the information and put it on the *hard drive* in your brain, so when you need a personal story to make a point, you can grab and use that *file!*

Rhyming feels good to say and can be memorable.

- **Examples**:
  - » Use these *tools* to *gain* and *retain* clients.
  - » In this example, the word, *tools* is a metaphor. *Gain* and *retain* rhyme.

> » "We'll discuss the components, parts, and elements of a speech. I'll *name* them, *explain* them, and give some examples."
> » (I also got the *Rule of Three* in there, didn't I?)

Use Alliteration

- Alliteration is repeating the initial sounds in neighboring words or syllables.
- **Examples**:
  - » A great one is Dr. Martin Luther King's speech at the Lincoln Memorial, August 28, 1963. He looked to a day when people "will not be judged by the *color* of their skin, but by the *content* of their *character*.
  - » One I use in concluding one of my talks is, "Do *that*, and my prediction is *this!*"
  - » One written for a CEO's Holiday party was, "I want to *Toast* the *Team* that made this an exceptional year!
  - » Here's another you saw earlier when discussing presentation slides: "The text on the screen does not reinforce the message – it *competes, confuses,* and *complicates* it!"

Use Analogies

- An Analogy is a comparison between two different things to draw attention to some point of similarity.
- **Contrasts can make lines memorable.**
  - » Fat – thin
  - » Black - white
  - » Full - empty

- **Examples:**
  - » John Kennedy, on October 20, 2006, said, "If a free society cannot help the *many* who are *poor*, it cannot save the *few* who are *rich*."
  - » "During the break at my first Toastmasters Meeting, Paul and Mitch came over and introduced themselves. *Instantly*, these *new* people in my life were like *old* friends."
  - » The *last* thing you say will be the *first* thing they remember!
  - » *Lying* to the Feds is like *tugging* on Superman's cape!
  - » Take a *complex* speech, and break it into *simple* steps.

Set up the Quotable Quote!

If your quote is not set up it will not have the desired affect. Here are some set up examples:

- "Let me leave you with this final thought . . ."
- "As you go to your warm home this evening, I'd like you to think about. . ."
- "One more thing . . ." (Steve Jobs, Apple Computer, has made this almost a signature part of his presentations at huge Apple events when introducing new products and services.)

Use these tips in crafting your Quotable Quote, and my prediction is this:

Your quote *will* be: Absolutely – Positively – There's no doubt in my mind - *That* quote *will* be – *Quotable!*

Answering Questions

Your presentations don't always need a **Question and Answer Session**. It may not be necessary or appropriate.

You may want to suggest that if people have questions, they see you after the talk or email you. This should come with the disclaimer that you will attempt to respond to as many as is reasonably possible.

You may be delivering the type of talk that is continually interactive with the audience. Often, **workshops** fall into this type of presentation.

Time Management is extremely important in any presentation.
- Taking and answering questions takes time management to a higher level.
- There is usually a specific amount of material to be covered.
- Long questions and long answers can throw a wrench into covering the scheduled material.
- Questions and answers that go off subject are even worse because they waste time that can't be recouped.

The Key to Time Management is this:
- Know exactly **What Material** has to be covered.
- Break that material into **Manageable Segments**. **Here is a suggestion:**
  - » Use timers with bells that ring at specific intervals. They can be used to start and mark the end of Q&A Sessions, specific segments of the workshop, break periods, and starting periods. It's a way of putting the timing into the

hands (clock hands!) of a third party. It does take good planning and practice to do this correctly.

Nearly everyone has attended workshops where twenty-five percent or more of the material didn't get covered adequately because of poor time management by the presenter. This is a *terrible* situation. It means justice hasn't been served to the audience or the presenter. Since time is usually controlled by the presenter, and everything wasn't presented, there is a less likely chance of the audience **Getting It!**

One interesting way **to handle questions is to have people** *write them down and hand them* **to you before going on break.**

- This gives the presenter the opportunity to be selective and pick the ones he wants to answer, and ignore the ones inappropriate or too time-consuming to be addressed.
- Questions not answered at the presentation can be answered by email or; the question and answer can be posted on your web site.
- This last idea is a great way of furthering the value you give.

The place in your talk that you *don't want a Question and Answer Session* **is at the end or after your closing.** That is *absolutely the worst time* to answer questions.

Remember the Law of Primacy and Recency. If Q&A is the *last* thing done before the audience leaves, it will be one of the *first* things they remember.

You don't have the control over Q&A that you have in the rest of your talk. Questions that are negative to your presentation, not easy to answer, or question (overtly challenge) something you presented, are not things you want uppermost in people's minds as they head for the exit.

The place to have questions asked is *before the conclusion of your talk*. Say something like this: "Before I conclude my talk, I'll take a few questions."

Additionally, let your audience know about this is in the **Opening** of your talk. This is where you tell the audience *what you're going to tell them*. Before getting into the Body of your speech, you say, "Before concluding my talk, there will be some time for questions. You may find them covered before that time. If not, please hold them until we set aside time to answer them."

If there are more questions than time, you can use one of the above suggestions and talk to people after the speech or accept emailed questions.

If you ask for questions and don't immediately get hands raised, you might have to *prime the pump*. A way to get things rolling is to say, "Typically, one of the questions I'm often asked is, _____ "

Always have a few of these in your hip pocket.

You might also plant a question with someone in the audience. One person raising their hand to a question usually leads to others doing the same.

Sometimes, I'll ask the first question to the audience.

Example: "Did you **GET IT**? If you **Got It**, please give me one takeaway from this presentation."

If you don't know the answer to a question there are several things you can do.

- Tell them you'll get back to them.
- Tell them to please see you after the presentation. You can then talk to them privately about the matter.
- Ask the audience, "Can anyone here respond to this?"
- Be honest. If you don't know the answer, tell them you don't.
- A softer way to answer, from your perspective, is to say, "I'm drawing a blank on that right now. When this brain cramp goes away, I'll get back to you."

Don't give an answer that you know is incorrect. Someone in the audience will know it's wrong and you lose credibility quickly.

Anticipate specific questions
- This is important because you can be ready with answers.
- You'll do a better job of giving the correct answer and give it more succinctly, if you've anticipated the questions you're likely to be asked and the appropriate answers.

Hints
- **Repeat the Question**, especially in a large room where each question is not spoken into a microphone.
- Look directly at the questioner as you start to answer it, then look at others in the audience so they don't feel they're not receiving your attention. While doing this check their temperature to confirm they're **GETTING IT!**

A Q&A Period can be included in your presentation. Like the other parts of a good presentation, this should be prepared and planned for.

21 Tips for Reducing the Fear of Public Speaking

First, if you have a Fear of Public Speaking - you are *not alone*.
As previously stated, it is one of the most common fears people have. There *is* comfort in knowing you're not the only person in the world who wouldn't jump at the chance to get in front of a group to deliver a talk.

Second, you really *don't* want to eliminate the Fear of Public Speaking, entirely.
A bit of nervous anxiety, channeled into your speech, will make it a better one.

One of the things we talk about in Toastmasters is the butterflies in our stomachs. We *don't* want to get rid of them. We *do* want them to *fly in formation*.

Sometimes we can get too comfortable and lose our pizzazz. I recall a member of my Toastmasters Club whose delivery lost its punch as he became *too* comfortable in front on audience. He needed to do something to get out of his comfort zone to bring up the quality of his talk. Perhaps speaking in front of a different audience or picking a subject to speak about that he hadn't spoken on before would bring back the great speaker we once knew.

Here are some tips and techniques that work for reducing the Fear of Public Speaking.

1. Know the Material You're Presenting

- Having *Confidence in your Competence* goes a long way towards easing the fear of presenting. Keep this confidence by keeping your knowledge up-to-date. Do this, and update your material accordingly.
- Imagine your subject was video, and you stopped researching after the VHS format came out. How would you feel when someone holds up a Flip camera and points it at you?

2. Practice, Practice, Practice - Then, Practice Some More!

- The better you know your material and the more times you've presented it, the more relaxed you'll be.
- Confidence grows with each practice and presentation. As your confidence grows, the Fear of Public Speaking lessens. With experience comes proficiency!

3. Memorize and Rehearse Ad Nauseam

- Don't memorize the entire speech. Do this for your **Opening, Closing**, and any **sticky spots** in your presentation.
- If you find yourself stumbling over specific words and phrases - *change them* to something that has the same meaning, but is easier to "speak."

4. *Never* Tell Your Audience that You Are Nervous!

- Odds are, they won't notice. They *want* you to succeed and are glad it's *you*, and not *them* at the lectern.

- If you say you're nervous or unprepared for the talk, you are setting yourself up for possible failure. Announce something like that, and people will be looking for it, and it will become a self-fulfilling prophecy.
- In fact, *don't be too smooth* in your delivery.
  - » The audience will better relate to you if you're human and real (that is, like them) in your presentation.
  - » Some ancient Chinese pottery purposely had cracks made on the pottery pieces so people would not think they were made by machinery.
  - » I recall a well-known national speaker who was *too good*. It was almost as if he had an Off/On Switch located somewhere. He didn't come across to his audience as one of us.

5. Have a Mind Map of Your Talk

- Practice with it and take it to the lectern even if you think you won't need it.
- Because a Mind Map uses pictures, symbols, and very little text, it is often a better way to view your talk versus black and white text. This is especially true if nervous. Sometimes those written speech outlines become one large blur.
- The pictures and symbols will remind you of a specific part of your talk. If you've practiced, you *know your stuff,* and the icon will trigger your memory.

6. Notes

- If not a Mind Map, take notes with key words highlighted to the lectern.
- Notes are best used by sliding the top page, when completed,

to the bottom of the other pages rather than having them stapled or paper clipped together and turning them. This makes their use less distracting.

- If more than one page, or using index cards, have them *numbered* in case you drop them. I've seen this happen, and it's *not* a pretty sight.

- Another tip for using index cards is to have a hole punched in the upper left hand corner and keep them together using a metal ring. This is especially effective if you walk and talk.

- There's a great story about Sir Winston Churchill and the use of notes. A reporter was interviewing the great statesman and asked, "Mr. Churchill, Sir. You are one of the world's greatest orators. I see you take notes to the lectern, but I rarely see you use them. Please explain." Sir Winston's reply was, "I carry homeowner's insurance, but I don't expect a fire!"

- I also like the way the motivational speaker Les Brown uses notes. He has the lectern at one side of the stage and turns it at a slight angle to the nearest outside corner. His notes are placed on it, and he goes towards the center of the stage to speak. When necessary, and he does it throughout his talk, he pauses (a *good* thing because it gives time for the audience to absorb his message), walks to the lectern, checks his notes, then walks toward his delivery location to continue is speech. He does this so naturally that it's very effective.

7. Breathe Your Way Calm

- When you breathe out, you relax. That's why people sigh when they're stressed. (That sigh does make you feel better, doesn't it?)

- Breathing in, without breathing out, causes hyperventilation and worsens anxiety.
- **Breathing Exercises:**
  » Just before your talk, take five minutes breathing *in* while counting to seven, and *out* to the count of eleven (quick count, not seconds!) Breathe out thru your mouth while making an "Ah" sound. On the out breath, hold it a second before breathing in again. This will produce quick and lasting calm. Extending the out breath calms you down.
  » Sometimes it helps to fill your belly with air, then gently push on your diaphragm as you exhale until all the air is out. Feeling the tension leave with this exercise can be extremely effective. Try it *now!*
  » Use the Japanese Jin Shin Jyutsu healing technique, of holding your index finger by wrapping the opposite hand around it, while you do the deep breathing. This may enhance, and quicken your relaxation.

8. Look Good!
- Check yourself in the mirror *before* getting introduced and going to the lectern.
  » It's not a bad idea to have a small hand mirror with your notes, computer, or something else that's with you at all presentations.
- Be sure buttons are buttoned, zippers zipped, no food between your teeth or on your face, hair combed, and no stains on your clothing.
- The last thing you need is people staring or laughing at you for one of these foibles.

9. Get a Good Night's Sleep.

- Being tired will negatively affect your presentation. You need energy to convey your message, and a good night's sleep before a speech will help immensely.

10. Check Your Meds!

- Since I just mentioned to avoid being sleepy, check your medications; prescription and nonprescription, for any side effects like drowsiness or dry mouth.
  - » If possible, take those pills *after* your presentation to avoid unwanted side effects.

11. Will the audience be able to see you?

- Check the line of sight from different audience positions.
  - » I've seen people seated behind posts and awkwardly leaning to see the speaker. *Remove* those seats!
- I've also seen presenters completely rearrange seating to fit their style, even going from traditional classroom seating to a semicircular seating arrangement.
  - » *Knowing* they'll see you will reduce stress.

12. Will they be able to hear you?

- Check out the PA system if you'll be using one.
- Meet, and become friends with, the audio visual person.
- *Knowing* they'll hear you will reduce anxiety.

13. What is the lighting like?

- Check ceiling, spotlight, *and* window lighting sources.
- Can the house lights be brought up or down?

- Who will be operating the spotlight?
- Assuring yourself lighting will not be a problem is one less thing to worry about.
- If window light and the direction of the sun could be a problem, are there curtains or shades, do they work, and who will draw them if necessary?
- **If they can't see you well**, they'll miss the important *nonverbal* parts of your presentation. If there is a disconnect between verbal and nonverbal communications, the nonverbal wins. Those who *see and hear* the speaker could get a different message from those who merely *hear* the talk. (Remember the Kennedy-Nixon Debate.)
- If they can't see you well, they'll get restless and become distractions themselves!

14. Try to Address All the Above *Before* Your Speaking Event.
- Lowering *potential* stress will lower *your* stress!

15. Arrive Early and Scope the Place Out.
- Where would any potential distractions come from?
- Check for kitchen doors, servers' wait stations, adjacent meeting rooms, street noise, etc.
  - » Eliminating outside distractions *before* you present will have a calming effect.
- Be certain everything from your checklist is set up and working the way it is supposed to. You *don't* want any last minute surprises that add tension.

16. Arrive Early to Meet and Greet!

- Introduce yourself to people coming to hear you. Ask their name and try to find out a little about them - things like what they do, why they came, and what they hope to learn.
  - » It's much easier to talk and connect emotionally to people you've already met and will dramatically reduce your anxiety.
- *This* suggestion is HUGE for reducing the Fear of Public Speaking! *Do It!*

17. Name Tags - *Insist on them.*

- We just talked about the importance of arriving early and *Meeting and Greeting* attendees as they arrive.
- The most important name is *our own!*
  - » Addressing someone by name while extending your hand is a quick and great way to meet those who came to see and hear you. It's also helpful, if your presentation is interactive, to be able to call upon and answer participants by name.
  - » **Name Tags** accelerate this and make it easier and more enjoyable.
  - » **Name Tags** invite you in, and close the distance between people.
  - » For *Meeting and Greeting* they *reach out* - and *pull you in!*
- **Name Tags** save people from embarrassing moments and help expand relationships and networks.
- *Picture this:* You walk into a room and two of five people are wearing **Name Tags**. Who do you introduce yourself to first?
- In advance of your presentation, find out if people will

be wearing **Name Tags**. If not, bring your own and a black Sharpie. (I keep both in my car!)

18. Exercise

- Running, brisk walks, biking and other physical activity are good ways to lessen stress.
- Some people do isometrics, possibly with a squeeze ball, before speaking.

19. Beta Blockers

- These are doctor prescribed medications that lower anxiety.
- Consult your physician to determine if these would be a fit for you. Some find them very helpful at first, and eventually don't need them.

20. Hypnosis

- For some individuals, this could be a method of relaxation worth looking into.
- Do some research and check references to find a practitioner who has experience in the area.

21. *Always* Remember . . .

- I know I'm repeating myself, but your audience *wants* you to be successful! They are mentally pulling for you, and usually glad *they* are not delivering the talk.

Check Out This Presenter's Check List!

Expecting the unexpected is a necessary step for having a successful presentation.

When it happens during your presentation, the effect could be the audience won't **GET IT!**

Having your audience **GET IT!** is the goal of all communication; written, spoken, or visual.

First: Have a list.
What to Double Check and What Could Go Wrong

Next: Work your way thru the list, fixing what needs to be fixed and having plans for what could happen.

Here's The List

Sound system
- Microphone(s), yours and audience participation one(s)
- Microphone feedback
  - » Extra battery if required

» Know where the on/off switch is
» If a mounted microphone, and necessary, adjust the distance

Audio Speakers
• Amplifier and controls working

Lighting
• Lighting on you
• Audience lighting
• Ability to lower and turn off

Distracting noise from
• Outside; parking lot, street, air (could be near an airport)
• Other meetings and adjoining rooms
• Hallway
• Kitchen
• Server wait stations
• Backstage

Visual
• Props
• Must be easily accessed and easy to put away after used

PowerPoint presentations
• Computer and backup plan
• Mouse and transmitter (if wireless)
• Test the settings on the computer to see that the projection screen gives the resolution needed *before* the presentation.

- Projector and backup plan (spare bulb)
- Projection screen; fixed or powered
- Remote control (hopefully with a **B Button**)
- Backup plan if PowerPoint can't be delivered
- If you've customized your slideshow, double check that you bring the correct one and not one customized for another presentation
- Power strip(s) (have your own, just in case)
- Electrical adapters
- Extension cord (have your own, just in case)

Room where presentation will be
- Temperature and ability to adjust easily
- Location of rest rooms (further away requires a longer break)
- Doors that access the room (sometimes there may be doors that directly exit the building)
- Seating; classroom, semicircle, or ?
- Pillars and/or other things (audio visual stands) that could block audience seeing you and vice-versa
- Backdrop; what is behind you and could it be a distraction
- Windows
- Can they be closed and curtains drawn over them to keep light out

Personal
- Water for yourself (room temperature – suggestion: bring your own bottle)
- Place to put change, keys and other items you might carry
- Location of rest room for last minute mirror check

- Copy of your presentation
- Name tag for yourself
- Name tags for attendees (if the meeting planner didn't take care of this)
- Black Sharpie for printing on the Name Tags
- Business cards
- Copy of introduction emcee will be using to introduce you

Have a *Plan B* if. . .
- If the emcee doesn't ask everyone to put their cell phones and pagers on STUN!
- Probably best you ask them to turn them off. Audience members looking at emails and text messages can be very distracting to you *and* others in the audience.
- All the speakers don't show, and your speech is moved up in time
- A speaker goes *over* their allotted time and you must cut the time of your talk
- A speaker goes significantly *under* their allotted time and the meeting planner wants you to extend your presentation.
- The demographics of the audience weren't quite what you thought they would be
- Parts of your presentation may now be inappropriate

Be certain to
- Know who is speaking before you and what their talk will be about
- Know who is speaking after you and what their talk will be about

- If you're going to have handouts (advised only if used as a workbook) be sure you have enough copies
- Other things to know
- Who to call for immediate help if something goes wrong and how to get ahold of them
- Possible attendees who should be recognized from the platform

Use The List!

Quotes on Public Speaking & Presentations

I collected a variety of quotes on the topic of this book and wanted to share them with you.

"Words are, of course, the most powerful drug used by mankind."
- Rudyard Kipling

"They may forget what you said, but they will never forget how you made them feel."

- Carl W. Buechner

"There are three things to aim at in public speaking: first, to get into your subject, then to get your subject into yourself, and lastly, to get your subject into the heart of your audience"

- Alexander Gregg

"There are always three speeches for every one you actually gave. The one you practiced, the one you gave, and the one you wish you gave."

- Dale Carnegie

"Mere words are cheap and plenty enough, but ideas that rouse and set multitudes thinking come as gold from the mines."
- A. Owen

"All the great speakers were bad speakers at first."
- Ralph Waldo Emerson

"The real art of conversation is not only to say the right thing at the right place but to leave unsaid the wrong thing at the tempting moment."
-Dorothy Nevill

"Make sure you have finished speaking before your audience has finished listening."
- Dorothy Sarnoff

"Many attempts to communicate are nullified by saying too much."
- Robert Greenleaf

"No one ever complains about a speech being too short!"
- Ira Hayes

"Always be shorter than anybody dared to hope."
-Lord Reading, on speech making

"Words ought to be a little wild for they are the assaults of thought on the unthinking."
- John Maynard Keynes

"Broadly speaking, the short words are the best, and the old words best of all."

- Sir Winston Churchill

"You can speak well if your tongue can deliver the message of your heart."

-John Ford

"Words have incredible power. They can make people's hearts soar, or they can make people's hearts sore."

- Dr. Mardy Grothe

"There are two types of speakers, those that are nervous and those that are liars."

- Mark Twain

"The best way to sound like you know what you're talking about is to know what you're talking about."

- Author Unknown

Speech is power: speech is to persuade, to convert, to compel."

-Ralph Waldo Emerson

"Courage is what it takes to stand up and speak; courage is also what it takes to sit down and listen."

- Winston Churchill

"Be still when you have nothing to say; when genuine passion moves you, say what you've got to say, and say it hot."
- D. H. Lawrence

"The right word may be effective, but no word was ever as effective as a rightly timed pause."
- Mark Twain

"It's not how strongly you feel about your topic, it's how strongly they feel about your topic after you speak."
-Tim Salladay

"The most precious things in speech are the pauses."
- Sir Ralph Richardson

"Well-timed silence hath more eloquence than speech."
- Martin Fraquhar Tupper

"A good orator is pointed and impassioned."
- Marcus T. Cicero

"Let thy speech be better than silence, or be silent."
- Dionysius Of Halicarnassus

"It takes one hour of preparation for each minute of presentation time."
- Wayne Burgraff

"There are certain things in which mediocrity is not to be endured, such as poetry, music, painting, public speaking."

- Jean de la Bruyere

"Say not always what you know, but always know what you say."

- Claudius

"If you would be pungent, be brief; for it is with words as with sunbeams - the more they are condensed, the deeper they burn."

- Robert Southey

Conclusion

Now it's time to conclude *my* writing, and for *you* to start speaking.

So let me end this book where we started.

The **Goal of all Communication** - verbal, written, or visual - is the same. We want the recipient(s), quickly as possible, to **GET IT!** They may not agree with any, or even all your message, but unless they **GET IT!**, there cannot be a meaningful discussion going forward.

We discussed the fact that you don't have to make presentations, or do public speaking, to benefit from the skills and confidence you'll acquire learning to do them. It usually is the process, not the event, isn't it? It's definitely that way with speaking. I've seen, and experienced, the paybacks.

It will help your career by putting you before people as an expert and a leader. The increased self-confidence of processing these skills will have a carryover effect to other areas of your life.

There is, in my mind, no skill more important than communication. You can be the world's leading authority on a subject and be extremely enthusiastic about it. However, if you're unable to present to an audience in a manner that educates, entertains and explains your subject, they won't **GET IT!** If they don't **GET IT!**, you probably won't be seen as the Expert you are, and your career will not reap the benefits of your knowledge.

We talked about developing, practicing, and delivering a speech. Mind Mapping, a nonlinear brainstorming tool, is something I've used for years and is well-worth learning.

(Learn more at www.mastermindmapper.com)

We reviewed the components, parts, and elements of a speech in some detail, and gave examples along the way.

We also discussed techniques and tips that will enhance your presentations and make them more memorable.

I'll conclude this book, as I conclude my keynotes and workshops, and that's with a **Challenge** and a **Prediction**.

My challenge to you is this:

The next time you're offered the opportunity to speak... Let's revise that to: *Find that opportunity!*

Seek it out! Find it where you work. Find it at your trade association, church, civic group, or any club you belong to.

Seek it out... Find it... and *Grab it!*

Then, develop, practice, and deliver that speech using all the components, parts, and elements of *No Sweat* Public Speaking!

Do *that* and my prediction is *this:*

Your speech will be:

Absolutely,
Positively,
There's *No Doubt in my Mind.,*

No Ifs, Ands, or Buts about it ...

That speech will be *—No Sweat!*

Bonus Offer

I've mentioned what a super tool Mind Mapping can be for Developing, Practicing, and Delivering a speech.

To this end, I have developed several templates you'll find extremely helpful for your Speaking activities.

These templates include the *No Sweat* Public Speaking! Formula Template, Speech Development Template, Speech Delivery Template, and Subject Development Template. Additionally, there are templates for Strategic Planning, Problem Solving, Decision Making, and a variety of other Brain Related Activities. There is also a template with links to many great sites that will help you with words, ideas, quotations, and other information relevant to Developing, Practicing, and Delivering that great speech of yours.

One of the many values of the Mind Mapping software and templates is the ability to easily customize it for your own use, link to specific URLs, documents, and other Mind Maps. The value of these templates is $225.00. Inspiration software, the Mind Mapping software I've used for years, is $75.00.

As a bonus to *No Sweat* Public Speaking! readers, I've bundled the templates, *with* the software for a very special price. Go to www.nosweatpublicspeaking.com/softwarebonus and put in the code TEMPLATES.

If you own Inspiration software, I've got a special offer for the Templates only.

Go to www.nosweatpublicspeaking.com/softwarebonustermplates and put in the code TEMPLATES ONLY.

A portion of the sale of each copy of *No Sweat* Public Speaking! will be donated to:

SmileTrain
CHANGING THE WORLD
ONE SMILE AT A TIME

WHY?

In the chapter about nonverbal communication, Facial Expressions were one of the elements. The most universal facial expression is a smile. I refer to a smile as a non-physical hug. The analogy is this: When you give one – you usually get one right back.

Can you imagine not being able to smile at someone? That's the least problem for those individuals suffering from cleft lip and palate. The presence of a cleft lip or cleft palate is a major problem in developing countries where there are millions of children affected and unable to afford surgical repair. Most cannot eat or speak properly, aren't allowed to attend school or hold a job, and face very difficult lives filled with shame and isolation, pain, and heartache. Their parents are so poor; they could never afford surgery. So they wait, and they hope, and they pray that someday, someone will come along and help them.

You could be that someone.

It costs as little as $250 to give a desperate child not just a new smile, but a new life.

What Makes The Smile Train Different:
- They are focused on a single problem: cleft lip and palate.
- They *teach* a man to fish: they empower local doctors in developing countries.
- They offer the lowest cost per surgery of any cleft charity.
- They have the best safety and quality record amongst cleft charities.
- They bring your donations to the poorest countries on earth which magnifies the impact.
- They help children in 77 of the world's poorest countries.

Learn more at: http://www.smiletrain.org

Changing The World One Smile At A Time.

Suggested Further Readings

Present Yourself!: *Capture Your Audience with Great Presentation Skills* by Michael Gelb

The Sir Winston Method: *The Five Secrets of Speaking The Language of Leadership* by James C. Humes

Podium Humor: *A Raconteurs's Treasury of Witty and Humorous Stories* by James C. Humes

Speaker's Library of Business Stories, Anecdotes and Humor by Joe Griffith

Smart Speaking: *60-Second Strategies for More Than 100 speaking Problems and Fears* by Laurie Schloff and Marcia Yudkin

The Speaker's Sourcebook: *Quotes, Stories and Anecdotes for Every Occasion* by Glenn VanEkeren

Gene Perret's **Funny Business:** *Speaker's Treasury of Business Humor for All Occasions* by Gene Perret and Linda Perret

On Writing Well: *The Classic Guide to Writing Nonfiction* by William Zinsser

Influence: *Science and Practice* by Robert B. Cialdini

Artful Persuasion: *How to Command Attention, Change Minds, and Influence People* by Harry Mills

Presentation Zen: *Simple Ideas on Presentation Design and Delivery* by Garr Reynolds

Trainer's Bonanza: *Over 1000 Fabulous Tips & Tools* by Eric Jensen

The Mind Map Book: *How to Use Radiant Thinking to Maximize Your Brain's Untapped Potential* by Tony Buzan and Barry Buzan

Get Ahead: Mind Map Your Way to Success by Vanda north and Tony Buzan

Idea Mapping: *How to Access Your Hidden Brain Power, Learn Faster, Remember More, and Achieve Success in Business* by Jamie Nast

Mapping Inner Space: *Learning and Teaching Mind Mapping* by Nancy Margulies

About the Author

Fred E. Miller is an author, speaker and coach.

For over forty years he has been a successful entrepreneur owning or partnering in a number of successful businesses.

After a short stint with Proctor & Gamble, he started a Coffee Service in Carbondale, Illinois. A year and a half later, he sold it and returned to his home town, St. Louis, Missouri where he bought into a boyhood friend's Coffee business. Eventually, they had a friendly split and Fred merged his portion with a former competitor. He left that industry after about thirty-five years and bought a local Sales Lead Service where he provided business prospecting services. He sold this enterprise several years later.

He then became an independent business developer and specialized in helping companies gain and retain clients, and sell more products and services to them.

Fred's business passions are Public Speaking/Presentations and Mind Mapping.

His Public Speaking passion goes back over forty years to the first time he heard Zig Ziglar, the famous motivational speaker. That talk, and those of other professionals who spoke for a living, made a lasting impression upon him of the power a speaker can have on an audience.

Fred was in Toastmasters for many years and served a term as president of his club.

During his time in Toastmasters he attended an International Convention and was introduced to Mind Mapping, a nonlinear, visual brain storming tool. Immediately this clicked with him and soon became a passion.

Those two passions, Mind Mapping and Public Speaking, go hand in glove.

Public Speaking is one great way to gain credibility and advance a career. Mind Mapping is the perfect tool for developing, practicing and delivering those presentations.

Fred's had the opportunity to speak at local, regional and national meetings.

Fred E. Miller is available for Keynotes, Workshops and Coaching.

Fred E. Miller
Fred@NoSweatPublicSpeaking.com
nosweatpublicspeaking.com
314-517-8772

 About the Illustrator

I'm sure you agree the illustrations in this book add significantly to the understanding of the Components, Parts and Elements of *No Sweat* Public Speaking! They also deepen the understanding of ways to lessen the Fear of Public Speaking and Tips for Improving Presentations.

David Zamudio was born in 1957 in St. Louis, Missouri and studied Fine Art and illustration at Washington University and Commercial art/design at the Graphique Art Institute in St. Louis.

Having received a certificate of excellence from The National Society of Arts and Letters for one his drawings, Zamudio continues his freelance illustration work.

David's illustrations and editorial cartoons have been featured in various publications including the St. Louis Post Dispatch, Suburban Journals, Best Bridal magazine and other local publications. International devotees and clients span the globe from Europe to Australia. Zamudio is also the founder of Zamudios Studio, an illustration and design company.

ZamudiosArtStudio.com
(314) 422-6492
info@zamudiosartstudio.com   www.zamudiosartstudio.com

About the Designer

We're all familiar with the expression, "Don't judge a book by it's cover."
The fact is, *we do!*
This book looks GREAT, *really GREAT!*
It looks GREAT because it had a GREAT DESIGNER - Sarah Barrie, Business Couture.
When it comes to Public Speaking and Presentations, I know a lot. I know very little about book design, layout, production, etc.
Sarah is an EXPERT in these areas. If were not for her expertise, guidance and considerable patience, this project would never be the quality

you experienced.

As stated in my chapter about the Title of your Speech, your Title should be something that will grab a potential audience's attention and make them want to know more. The cover, and interior design of this book does that - *doesn't it?* It does it because Sarah made it happen!

She has been an absolute delight to work with, and I highly recommend her services to anyone having the same goal I have - a beautiful, published Book!

Sarah can be contacted through her website: www.bizcouture.com

CPSIA information can be obtained
at www.ICGtesting.com
Printed in the USA
LVOW01s2339230616

493930LV00008B/29/P